English Series
General *Editor*—ERNEST BERNBAUM

BEOWULF

AND

SIR GAWAIN AND THE GREEN KNIGHT

BEOWULF

AND

SIR GAWAIN AND THE GREEN KNIGHT

*Poems of Two Great Eras
with Certain Contemporary Pieces*

Newly Translated by
GORDON HALL GEROULD
Professor of English, Princeton University

THE RONALD PRESS COMPANY
NEW YORK

Library of Congress Catalog Card Number: 53-11212

PRINTED IN THE UNITED STATES OF AMERICA

CONTENTS

BEOWULF 9

CYNEWULF 103
    An Advent Hymn 104
    Constantine's Vision and Battle with the
        Huns 105

THE WANDERER 110

THE VISION OF PIERS PLOWMAN 114

THE AUTHOR OF *The Pearl* AND *Sir Gawain* . 126
    The Pearl 127
    Sir Gawain and the Green Knight . . . 132

NOTES 201

PREFACE

AT TWO periods previous to the sixteenth century writers of English composed works of major importance: poems of such merit in each case that they were unrivalled at the time in other European literatures and have never lost their power to stimulate the minds and imaginations of readers. This happened in the eighth century and again in the latter half of the fourteenth century. The translations in this little book have been made with the hope of showing something of the interest and beauty to be found in what men wrote during these two great eras.

We know all too little, it must be confessed, about why one period produces authors of exceptional genius and another merely writers of moderate gifts. The fact remains that sometimes the giants appear. That there must be hidden causes no one can doubt, but the best we can do is to study the works of these giants and try to understand why they have not grown old with the passage of time. The more carefully we read them, the more pleasure we can get, because we can increasingly adjust ourselves to the point of view of their authors, see as they saw, feel as they felt. Understanding great books is a step towards understanding life itself, and should help to illuminate all human experience. They should be read with that in view—not as specimens from a museum of history.

The eighth century in England was more unlike the fourteenth than is the twentieth. The Anglo-

Saxons were not far removed from the tribal life out of which they had emerged. They had not achieved political unity, and they still felt and acted according to instincts that were the result of immemorial racial experience. They had recently accepted Christianity, however, and with it the educated few in the Church and at the royal courts had absorbed to a remarkable degree the learning of the ancient world as it had been transmitted through Rome and the Celts of Ireland. This combination of cultures somehow stimulated the more gifted poets among them to the production of a literature fresh in insight, dignified in form, noble in spirit. What they wrote was steeped in the two-fold tradition they had inherited, but it was also the beginning of modern poetry. *Beowulf* is its magnificent representative.

In the second half of the fourteenth century the Middle Ages were drawing to a close. The feudal pattern of society, the codes of chivalry, and the organization of learning and religion that had been worked out during the preceding centuries were still flourishing; but they were being undermined by new forces. Literature and learned studies had already changed their direction in Italy; there was an increased national consciousness; exploration and trade had tapped new sources of wealth, with a consequent rise to power of the merchants; unrest with old forms and old abuses was threatening as never before. In England, though not elsewhere in Europe except for the earlier Italian, this ferment resulted in a brief outburst of literary energy that produced Geoffrey Chaucer and such contemporaries as John Gowrr, Wiclif, and the authors of *Piers Plowman* and *Sir Gawain and the Green Knight*. Within fifty years they gave to England and to us so many works of lasting value that we look back on the period of their activity as the second great era in our literature. Chaucer, the most gifted of these men, is not represented in this volume partly because he deserves and requires a book to himself, and partly because he can be read, after a little study, without the aid of translation. But he should never be thought of as an isolated figure : he is best understood as the foremost writer of a fortunate time.

BEOWULF

"*Beowulf* occupies a unique position in the literature of Western Europe as the earliest poem of importance in any vernacular after the collapse of Roman civilization. It is the herald of modern letters, as the *Iliad* and the *Odyssey* are of classical letters, and it is not unworthy of comparison with those earlier and greater epics. Like them, it reflects the manners and ideals of an age which may with some propriety be called 'heroic.' Its chief adventures are as fantastic as any in the wanderings of Ulysses, yet its historical background affords an unrivalled picture of the early life of our pagan ancestors. Political and social conditions are as vividly and as truthfully set forth as if there were no demons lurking in the mists at nightfall, no dragon watching on the windy heights. But the main importance of a great poem must lie in its poetry. As to this, no apologies for *Beowulf* are necessary. The tale itself and the traditions encircling it have all the authority of centuries of story-telling over ale-cups and by winter firesides. Then, in a happy hour, it became the theme of a gifted poet, and received its final epic form. Although it deals with the exploits of Scandinavian heroes, it is a thoroughly English poem, written in the English language, in a verse and style characteristically English, and infused with the spirit and ideals of English folk. There is every reason why we of to-day who have inherited those traditions should know *Beowulf*, and appreciate it as a work of art." (W. W. Lawrence, *Beowulf and Epic Tradition*, 1928, p. vii.)

Beowulf is thus not only the first great landmark in English literature, but the earliest representative of the new civilization that gradually emerged in Europe after the barbarian invaders from the North had begun to absorb what was left of Roman culture. To the best of our knowledge, it was written in the early years of the eighth century. During the previous hundred years the Anglo-Saxons had been christianized by missionaries from Rome and Ireland, and with the new religion had taken over such learning as had survived the collapse of the ancient world. The author of *Beowulf* was a contemporary of Bede, who was internationally famous as a scholar though he lived in a monastery close to the northern border of England. He was a contemporary also of poets who put into verse very like his own, stories from the Old Testament. Both he and they, though Christians and probably clerics, had not forgotten the barbarian traditions of their race, which accounts for the strange but appealing mixture in their work of elements from two widely different cultures. All of them worshipped God, but they remembered Wyrd as the shaper of man's destiny; they had learned to read Latin poetry, as they had learned to write in Roman letters, but they composed in a style and metre peculiar to themselves.

The epic form in which the *Beowulf* poet cast his materials owed something to both traditions. There is no evidence that the lays recited by Germanic minstrels in pagan times had the same broad scope and sweep of narrative. Although we cannot be sure of this, since none of the poetry of pre-Christian days has survived unaltered, it seems probable that the author of *Beowulf* knew about Virgil's *Æneid,* even if he had not read it, and thus learned from the classical epic how to enlarge upon his theme and give it the elevation of tone it possesses. Yet his background of tradition and the ways of men he was depicting were so different from those of the ancient world that he made something quite new—an heroic poem no less vigorous and no less noble in spirit than earlier epics, and, though lacking in the same refinement of artistry, surpassing them in moral value.

His theme was the deeds of a man who personified the virtues as they were understood at the time: physical and moral courage, loyalty to rulers and equal loyalty to followers, generosity of spirit and lavishness with possessions, scorn of what was mean. Beowulf's prowess is the unifying element, to which everything else is subordinated, just as all the other characters are subordinated to him. It has sometimes been said that the poem has no real unity, but is a mere grouping of three episodes from the life of the hero. Any such statement is based on a misconception not only of *Beowulf* but of epic poetry in general. In the *Odyssey* and the *Æneid,* for example, we do not find a story told straightforwardly from the first event to the last. In order to get boldness of design and amplitude of execution, qualities necessary to the effectiveness of heroic poetry, the action is compressed within a relatively brief period and is focussed on a relatively small number of events. Things supposed to have happened earlier are told reminiscently by one or another character, and certain future events are revealed by prophecy. In *Beowulf* the method is essentially the same, although it is true that the so-called third episode takes place fifty years after the adventures recounted in the earlier part of the poem. The point to be noted is that the author was trying to show the hero through the great deeds he performed—his whole life and character. He therefore centred attention on two representative actions, one of Beowulf's vigorous young manhood and one of his old age, developing each with fullness of detail and dramatic force. The Beowulf who went across the sea to rescue Hrothgar's land from the devastations of Grendel was the same man who met his death while rescuing his kingdom, so much later, from the ravages of the fire-breathing dragon. We should not know him properly unless we had these two varying illustrations of his courage and prowess. The last adventure, moreover, brings his life to a tragic and triumphant end, tragic because human intervention stirred the anger of the dragon and led it to the attacks which the hero gave his life to avenge, triumphant because the people of the Geats were saved though their lord perished. It is a magnificent conclusion to a splendid story.

Into the framework of the two adventures is fitted everything else about Beowulf that has any significance: his family history, his astonishing power as a swimmer, his relationships with other royal persons in different lands, his assistance of the kings under whom he served before he came to the throne of the Geats. Some of these things are told by the poet, some—like the swimming contest with Breca—by the hero himself. The story is enriched, moreover, by being set against a background in which are seen other heroes and other kings. To us, who know so imperfectly the history and legends of the Germanic tribes, this back-ground is somewhat bewildering in its detail, but it serves to give the proper atmosphere through which to see Beowulf's own deeds as a hero. Without them the story would lack perspective. We should be less able to comprehend how the Anglo-Saxons and the poet himself looked at what was worth while in life.

We cannot expect an epic to give us characters or actions with what we call, in connection with a modern novel, "truth to life." Everything is magnified and made to appear somewhat larger than actuality. Grendel is a monster of peculiarly terrible qualities, and Beowulf, to cope with him, must have the strength of thirty men in his hands. Yet the scenes are imagined so vividly and with such completeness that we get the feeling of reality throughout them. They may enlarge human actions, but they do not falsify them. The manners and customs pictured, moreover, are undoubtedly those observed by the poet or known to him from tradition. The Anglo-Saxons must have sailed the seas and guarded their coasts, must have feasted and mourned very much as the Geats and Danes are represented as doing. What is even more important, they certainly felt as the people in the poem feel. All in all, there is real truth to life in what we are shown, for otherwise it could not move us as it does after the passage of twelve centuries.

The metre and style of Beowulf, like that of most Old English poems, was one adapted to recitation or chanting. It abounded in bold metaphors, called kennings, and did not avoid stereotyped phrases, probably because the familiar sounds echoed pleasantly in the ears of the listeners. For the same reason, doubtless, there is a marked use of parallelism, the repetition of the same thought in different words— a device with which everyone is familiar in the *Book of Psalms*. Each line of Old English verse has four strong beats or accents, but the number of unstressed syllables varies widely. One of the stressed syllables in the second half of the line always alliterates with one or both of the stressed syllables in the first half. By this means an echo of sound is produced that serves somewhat the same purpose as rhyme. In the translation that follows, an effort has been made to reproduce these characteristic features of Old English poetry, though it is difficult to do this successfully because of changes in our language—notably the loss of inflectional endings. The translator can only hope to give the reader some inkling of the imaginative power that makes *Beowulf* no mere historical document but a living work of art.

We have heard of the Spear-Danes in the days
    of yore,
what glory came to the kings of the people,
the deeds of might of the doughty leaders.
    Often Scyld Scefing from the enemy tribes,
5 from many a clan their mead-halls took,
a terror to warriors, though a time there was

when he endured misery. Amends for it came,
and great under heaven he grew with his honors
till the peoples about must obey his words,
10 and each of the tribes must tribute pay
that dwelt by the sea. A doughty king!
To him a son was sent thereafter,
a gift of God for the good of the people,
a youth in the courts, who recalled the distress
15 that the leaderless folk full long had endured
in the days of old. Then honor gave
the Ruler of Life, the Lord of Glory,
to the son of Scyld; and resounded the praise
of Beowulf loud through the land of the Danes.
20 Let a young man like him take heed to do good
by splendid gifts from the store of his father,
that in age the people thereafter may serve him
as willing companions when war shall come,
may stand beside him; for such are the deeds
25 by which one thrives in tribes everywhere.
    Then Scyld fared forth in the faith of his Lord,
at the time appointed departed right old.
His dear companions down to the sea-brink,
as he had bidden, then bore their lord,
30 fulfilled the words of the friend of the Scyldings,
of their lord beloved, who long had reigned.
Gleaming and ready, a ring-prowed vessel
on the beach there stood, a ship for a hero.
They placed their prince, their precious ruler,
35 the giver of rings, in the roomy hull,
where he sat by the mast 'mid a mighty treasure
brought from afar, the famous king.
Never heard I of boat that better was laden
with the weapons of war and the weeds of battle,
40 with swords and with byrnies; and his bosom was
        covered

with the hoard of wealth that he was to carry
to the grasp of the flood as afar he departed.
Not less the gifts they gave to him then
of the people's treasure than those aforetime,
45 who sent him forth to find his way
alone on the waves, being weak and a child.
Now high they placed overhead a banner,
a golden standard; the sea they let take him,
to the ocean gave him; and grave were their hearts,
50 mournful their spirits.　Men have no knowledge,
no wit to tell us, though wise in the hall,
who received that burden or brought it to port.

　　In the camps of the Scyldings as king reigned
　　　　Beowulf;
dear lord of his people, for long he ruled,
55 and famed was afar when his father had gone,
the prince from the realm, till arose thereafter
Healfdene the mighty, who held while he lived,
fiercely battling till old, the happy Scyldings.
To him four sons were sent in turn,
60 as leaders in war awoke in the world,
Heorogar and Hrothgar and Halga the Good;
and a daughter, I heard, was Onela's queen,
bed-companion of the Battle-Scylfing.

　　To Hrothgar was given glory in battle,
65 acclaimed with such honor that his clansmen loyal
gladly obeyed him, and his band of youths
waxed great and mighty.　Then grew his heart eager
to build for himself a hall that was worthy,
a mead-hall mightier than men had known,
70 a dwelling that fitted the fame he had won;
and there within to the old and the young
what God had allotted he would give as was right,
save the rule of men and the realm that he held.
I have heard that the work through the world was
　　　　spread

75 among many a tribe to make the folk-hall
and adorn it fitly. It was done at his will,
and with speed was finished, spacious and lofty,
the greatest of halls. Hart he named it,
the ruler whose word so widely had power.
80 He forgot not his promise of giving out rings,
wealth at the feasting. Till the flames devoured it,
the high hall stood with horns on the gables,
towered lofty, for the time was not yet
when the direful hate of a daughter's spouse
85 should stir to malice and slaughter there.
But the monster who lurked in the lowering
shadows,
the mighty demon, endured it ill
when he heard each day the din and the revelry
that was loud in the hall. The harp resounded,
90 and the minstrel sang, reciting clearly
what well he had mastered of man's beginning,
how the All-Wielder had wrought the earth,
the smiling world which the sea surrounds,
in triumph had set the sun and the moon
95 as lights to illumine the landsmen's ways,
and every region of earth made fair
with limb and with leaf ; life, too, had given
to all of mankind who have ever had birth.
So the tribesmen lived long with rejoicing,
100 blessed and happy, till the hellish fiend
his crimes began, that creature damned.
The monster grim Grendel was named,
who kept to the moors and the murky fens,
defying all law. Long had he dwelt there,
105 the hapless creature in the haunt of demons,
condemned by the Lord and driven forth
for his kinship to Cain, who had killed his brother.
Avenged was Abel by the edict of God.

Who banished the slayer for the sin he had done
210 from the race of mankind, the Ruler of Heaven.
The sire he was, the source of all monsters,
the giants and elves and the goblins, too,
the fearsome tribes who fought for long
against God the Eternal. He gave them their due.
115   In the murky night came the monster to spy
on the Ring-Danes left in the lofty house
after the feasting, and he found therein
the band of æthelings bound in slumber,
full fed and asleep, all sorrows forgotten,
120 all woes of mankind. The wight of destruction
stern and greedy, stayed not his hand,
savage and fierce, but seized at their rest
some thirty thanes, and thence returned,
exultant hastened to his haunt in the moors,
125 dragging the spoil of the slaughter home.
As the light of morning lifted slowly,
the vengeance of Grendel was revealed to men;
there was sorrow at dawn, the sound of weeping
where the feast had been. The famous prince
130 sat unhappy and suffered dire grief,
the ætheling good for the thanes who had gone,
when once they had traced the track of the enemy,
the trail of the damned. Dreadful and tedious
the hateful war! Nor was it longer
135 than the very next night that the villain returned,
the creature to ravage, in crime relentless
and the wicked feud, bound fast in them.
Then many escaped, the men who could,
and sought their repose apart from the hall
140 in beds that they found in the bowers outside,
since the monster's hate was manifest there
by a visible sign. The survivors thus
were safer afar, as it seemed to them.

So wickedly ruled and unrighteously fought
40 one against all, until empty stood
the noblest of houses. And the havoc went on;
twelve winters' time the trusted Scylding
endured affliction and depth of woe,
encompassing sorrow, till it came to be known
150 to the children of men by means of their lays
that Grendel it was, grim and hostile,
who waged against Hrothgar a war relentless
bitter with hatred, a battle enduring
for many a season. With no man would he
155 of the Danish power make peace at all,
remove the menace, for money compound it;
nor could the elders in any wise hope
that compensation the slayer would pay.
A shadow dark, the death-dealing monster
160 lay ever in wait for age and for youth
from the lair that he held in the heavy dark
of the mist-laden moors. Men could not fathom
by what devious ways the demons would come.
Thus many a crime against man this enemy
165 direful and lonely did full often,
humbling afflictions; he haunted Heorot,
the splendid hall, in the shadows of night,
though never the throne and never the treasure
did the Lord let him nigh, Whose love he knew not.
170 Distressful was this, a trial of heart
to the friend of the Scyldings. Assembled often
the great of the kingdom, took counsel together
what best might be done by the doughty of heart
against the attacks that terror had brought.
175 Again they vowed at the fanes of their idol
and promised honors; prayers they offered
that the soul-destroyer might send them aid,
help their wretchedness, for heathen were they,

and such was their worship. They sought out hell
180 in the thoughts of their hearts, nor had heard of the
Lord
Who judges all men, the mighty God,
nor could praise as is right the Ruler of Heaven,
the Warden of Glory. Great woe is his
who in trouble dire must doom his soul
185 to the fiery pit, and can find no help
nor in any wise turn; but well is it with him
who shall seek at the day of his death the Lord
and find his peace in the Father's bosom.

Thus the son of Healfdene with sorrow continually
190 was stirred in his heart, for the hero, though wise,
could avert not the misery; too mighty the struggle,
hateful and tedious, that harrowed the people,
the grim distress, the greatest of night-ills.

Then heard in his home Hygelac's kinsman,
195 great among Geats, of Grendel's deeds.
Mighty he was, of men the brawniest,
of mortal heroes highest in power,
both strong and noble. 'Make ready a ship,'
he bade them, and said, a battle-king he
200 over the swan-road would seek out the prince,
the king so renowned who had need of men.
His prudent henchmen to hold him back
made little attempt, though beloved was he;
they praised the venture, and viewed the omens.
205 From the Geats the chieftain had chosen his warriors,
the keenest among them as comrades and friends.
With fourteen followers whom he found to his liking
he marched to the shore, to the ship that waited,
a mariner trained with his men behind him.
210 The hour had come; at the hill's base rode
the boat on the waves. The warriors mounted

the prow of the ship, while the surf came splashing,
sea against sand; they stowed their gear,
their weapons bright in the breast of the vessel,
215 their war-gear splendid. Then the warriors eager
pushed out the boat well-bound and sturdy.
Over the waters by the wind impelled
went the foamy-necked ship like a flying bird.
For a day it waded the deep unchecked,
220 the craft with its prow that was proudly uplifted,
until the sea-farers had sight of land,
the shore-cliffs steep, the shining nesses,
the mighty forelands. They had found their haven,
the voyage had ended. Then eagerly sprang
225 the folk of the Wethers forth on the land;
they moored the sea-wood; their stiff sarks rattled,
their garments of war; and God they thanked
for the prosperous faring they had found on the
        journey.
From the cliff by the shore the Scylding's sentinel,
230 who guarded the sea-wall, saw them bearing
over the bulwarks the bright-bossed shields,
the well-made armor; he wondered and questioned,
being eager to know who these aliens were.
Came riding, then, the thane of Hrothgar
235 down to the shore, and doughtily shook
the spear in his hands, and spoke as was fitting.
'What warriors are ye, weapon-bearers,
dressed in your corslets, who a ship high-keeled
over the sea-ways, over the ocean,
240 have hither brought? Long here have I been,
as guard of the coast have kept my watch
lest a hostile host do harm by a raid
on the land of the Danes down from their ships.
None more openly ever came hither
245 bearing their shields, though ye sought no leave

from the Danish clan, nor have claimed the right
by consent of the kinsmen. Never saw I on earth
a greater warrior than is one of you,
a hero in armor; no hall-thane merely,
250 if his looks deceive not, his splendid weapons,
his noble mien. Now must you tell me
what tribe you are from ere you farther move
as spies mayhap on the home of the Danes,
in doubtful ways. Far-dwellers, hear,
255 sea-wanderers, hearken; my words are plain;
it is best that quickly you break your silence,
declaring your race and whence you have come.'
   To him the leader unlocked his word-store,
gave him an answer the guide of the band:
260 'We are clansmen of the kin of the Geats,
hearth-companions of Hygelac's tribe.
My father was known to the folk full widely,
a noble war-leader whose name was Ecgtheow.
He lived many winters ere away he was reft,
265 old from our dwelling; and doubtless the wise
remember him well widely through earth.
We have come seeking the son of Healfdene,
thy lord, with hearts that are loyal and true.
We beg for thy counsel, since we have come hither
270 on a weighty errand to thy widely famed lord.
I make it known, since we need not conceal it,
as it seems to me. Instruct us, I pray thee,
if the rumor be true that has reached our ears
of something harmful, of hurt to the Scyldings,
275 of dire crimes done in the darkness of night,
of horror revealed and hurt unexampled,
of shameful murders. It may be to Hrothgar
my counsel might serve as a comfort to help him
in conquering this terror, overcoming the fiend,
280 if ever he find an end of affliction,

if trouble at length be turned away,
and the hot waves of care be cooled of their heat.
If not, then forever he must eke out wretchedly
a miserable life, while remains yet standing
285 on its lofty height the noblest of houses.'
　　The guardian spoke, where he sat on his steed,
the sentinel bold: 'The sharp-visioned warrior
whose thought is just must judge as of right
between words that are said and works that are done.
290 I now believe this a loyal band
to the lord of the Scyldings, and leave you to bear
your armor and weapons; I shall guide you.
Upon my companions I place the care
of your vessel here against hostile men,
295 your fresh-caulked ship that you leave on the sands,
to give it honor, till again it may bear
its dear lord returning o'er the deeps of the sea,
sharp-prowed and good, to the realm of the Geats,
should no harm be wrought in the rush of the battle
300 to him who will do deeds that are valorous.'
　　Then went they forth, while fast at anchor
stood in the offing their ship wide-bosomed.
Boar-figures glittered on golden helmets,
above the cheek-guards brightened and shone;
305 tempered by fire, talismans were they,
and guarded the men who moved together
and marched in haste till the timbered hall,
splendid with gold, they saw before them.
Most of renown known to earth-dwellers
310 was the stately hall where the high king sat;
the light of it shone over many lands.
Far off the soldier showed them the hall,
the dwelling resplendent of daring warriors,
made plain the pathway, then paused and said,
315 as he turned his steed: 'It is time for parting.
I go with the prayer that God Almighty

may guard and protect you by His guidance and
    grace,
keep you safe in your ventures! To the sea I must go
against hostile hosts to hold my watch.'

320 The street they followed with stones was bright,
and bright on the warriors the war-gear shone,
the ringed mail hard, hand-linked and burnished;
it sang as they moved, marching in order,
forth to the hall in fearsome array.

325 Sea-weary they set their broad shields down,
their bucklers strong, by the side of the dwelling;
they sank to the bench, their byrnies clanking,
the gear of the warriors; together they stood
their ashen shafts grey-tipped and sharp,

330 the seamen bold, for the band was armed
with splendid weapons. Then a warrior proud
questioned the heroes, asking their lineage:
'Whence bring ye, journeying, your bright-plated
    shields,
your hauberks gray, and your helmets forbidding,

335 a band with spears? I abide with Hrothgar,
his herald and servant. Saw I never
of foreign men so many or prouder.
Surely adventuring, not sent into exile,
in the pride of your hearts to Hrothgar you've come.'

340 Made answer straightway, strong-hearted and proud,
the prince of the Wethers in words like these,
bold under helmet: 'We are Hygelac's comrades
and do his bidding; Beowulf am I.
What errand I have to Healfdene's son,

345 to the prince renowned make known will I,
to thy lord if his grace will grant to us now
that we may approach his presence to seek.'
Wulfgar gave answer—of the Wendels a prince,
what manner of man was he to many was known,

350 how warlike and wise—: 'Of the warden of Danes,

the lord of the Scyldings, I will learn the will,
of the giver of rings, the glorious prince,
about thy coming, and bring thee again
some word in haste whether welcome thou art,
355 whatever may seem to my sovereign is right.'
Then he hurried and went where Hrothgar sat
very old and gray with a group of his warriors.
The brave man strode till he stood by the shoulder
of the king of the Danes; fit custom he knew.
360 Said then Wulfgar to his sovereign and friend:
'From afar journeying have fared to thee hither
over the waste of the ocean some warrior Geats.
His people call their captain and leader
by the name of Beowulf; and now they ask
365 that they, my prince, to thy presence may come
and have with thee speech. Withhold not from them
thine answer but grant it, O gracious Hrothgar!
Equipped are they well, and worthy they seem
of warriors' greeting; great in his power
370 is the chief who has brought the band of men hither.'
Returned answer Hrothgar, protector of Scyldings:
'I him recall. As a child I knew him.
His father was Ecgtheow, who found for a wife
by the gift of Hrethel—the Geat was he—
375 his only daughter. I deem that now
his brave son has come hither to seek his dear friend.
Men sailing hereby, bringing in friendship
to the tribe of the Geats gifts in their vessels,
have told me of him that his hand in its grip
380 of thirty men has the might and the power,
this battle-famed hero. Him the holy God
by His grace, as I hope, against Grendel's attacks
has hither sent to help and to aid us,
the Danes of the West. For his daring of heart
385 I shall offer gifts to the excellent hero.
Hasten therefore and have them enter

that the group of kinsmen together may greet me.
Assure them in words that welcome are they
to the Danish people.'   To the door of the hall
890 went Wulfgar and stood and spoke from the thresh-
          old:
'To you bids say my sovereign prince,
lord of the East-Danes, your lineage knowing,
that he welcomes you here from the waves of the sea
as brave-hearted men.   You may, then, enter
395 in your garments of war, wearing your helmets,
to look upon Hrothgar; but let your shields
await you here, and the wooden shafts
of your spears the outcome of the speech you shall
          have.'
      The leader arose and round him his band,
400 of the splendid troop all save a few
whom the chief commanded to remain with the gear.
They hastened together with the guidance of Wulf-
          gar
under Heorot's roof till the hardy leader,
bold in his helmet, on the hearth-stone stood.
405 Beowulf spoke—and his byrny shone,
his mail well wrought by the might of the smith:
'Hail thou, Hrothgar! I am of Hygelac
a thane and a kinsman, accustomed from youth
to deeds of greatness.   What Grendel has done
410 at home in my country came to my knowledge.
Sea-farers have it that this hall is standing
empty and idle, useless for all men,
though the noblest of buildings, after night has de-
          scended
and the evening light is lost from the firmament.
415 My people, therefore, the prudent and brave,
gave me the counsel that I should come,

Prince Hrothgar, and seek thee, having seen and
    known well
the strength of my might; remembering doubtless
what they themselves saw when, stained by my foes,
420 I came from the battle where five giants I bound,
destroyed their race, and slew in the waves
the shadowy dragons, enduring things dire
but avenging the Wethers who woe had suffered—
made an end of their enemy. And now against
    Grendel,
425 this monster alone I long to contend,
to finish the demon. Thus, lord of the Danes,
prince of Bright-Scyldings, one boon I would ask
if any favor I find with thee,
that thou wilt not forbid me, protector of warriors,
430 friend of thy folk, since afar I have come,
but let me cleanse with my clansmen alone,
this band of the hardy, Heorot hall.
This, too, I have learned, that leaving all weapons
the monster contends; so truly will I,
435 that my lord Hygelac may be happy of heart.
I will bear neither sword nor sheltering shield,
no buckler of yellow when the battle I enter,
but by the grip of my hands I will grasp at the foe,
contending thus only and trying my fate.
440 He whom death takes his trust must repose
in the Lord Who judges with justice mankind.
The demon will try, I doubt not, to eat
the folk of the Geats as before he devoured
oft in the hall, hesitant never,
445 the best of thy clansmen. No burial rites
needst thou give to my head, but he will have me
drenched with my gore if death shall be mine;
will make me a feast in the fen he inhabits,
will deluge with blood his den, and alone
450 ruthlessly eat me. Reck not of rites

to be done for my body. But if battle take me,
send to Hygelac the sark I wear,
best of war-gear, of garments the choicest,
an heirloom of Hrethel, a work of Weland.
455 Wyrd moves ever as Wyrd decrees.'
    Then spoke Hrothgar, helm of the Scyldings:
'Because of deeds that are past and duties that follow,
surely, friend Beowulf, thou hast sought us now.
Thy father began the greatest of feuds
460 when he struck Heatholaf and slew him of old,
of the tribe of the Wulfings; and the Wether folk
for fear of war failed to protect him.
In flight he sought the South-Dane people,
the Scyldings proud o'er the surge of the sea.
465 Then first I was ruling the folk of the Danes,
this rich city of heroes was holding in youth,
a widespread dominion. Dead was Heorogar,
had ceased to live the son of Healfdene,
my elder brother. He was better than I!
470 Later by payment I laid the feud,
sent to the Wulfings o'er the water's ridge
treasures ancient; oaths he swore to me.
Sorrow is it and sadness of heart
to tell to any the toll of shame
475 that Grendel has wrought by his grievous hate,
destruction in Heorot. My hall is diminished,
the band of my warriors. Wyrd has swept them
into Grendel's maw, but God may cut off
right well from his desperate deeds the destroyer.
480 Often boasted, when beer they had drunk,
my warriors fierce over flagons of ale
that they in the beer-hall would abide the coming
of Grendel's attack with the terror of swords.
Then was this mead-hall in the morning time,
485 the lordly room blood-stained, the benches all

moist with their life-stream when light came at
    length,
with the gore of battle. Gone were my dear ones,
my precious band loosened; I had lost them to death.
Now seat thyself, feast, and unseal to men
490 thy hoard of great deeds as thy heart shall incite.'
    Then in the beer-hall were benches made ready
for the men of the Geats together banded,
where strong of heart and stalwart in pride
they took their places. A retainer served them,
495 in his hand bearing a beaker adorned,
the sweet mead poured, while a poet sang
clear-voiced in Heorot. There was clamor of heroes,
a doughty assemblage of Danes and of Wethers.
    Then Unferth spoke, the son of Ecglaf,
500 who sat at the feet of the Scyldings' lord,
loosened his malice. Much vexation
was the bold sea-voyage of Beowulf to him,
for he did not wish that the world contain
another man who more of glory
505 achieved under heaven than he himself:
'Art thou the Beowulf who with Breca competed,
on the open sea in swimming contended,
ye two for pride proving the waters,
for a foolish boast braving the deeps
510 and risking your lives? From the rueful test
could neither friend nor foe dissuade you,
the pair of you set to swim in the sea.
You embraced the ocean, brandishing arms,
traversed the currents with the thrust of your hands,
515 through the whelming of waves away ever gliding,
through the wintry surge seven nights labored
in the waters' power. He surpassed you in swimming,
had greater might. In the morning time
he was cast on the beach of the Battling Reams,

520 whence he sought at length the land of the Brond-
        ings,
his country and home, where he held possession,
by the folk beloved, of a fair stronghold,
a city and treasures. Forsooth thus accomplished
the son of Beanstan his boasting to thee.
525 Thou wouldst find a worse outcome of the fighting
        fierce,
I am free to predict, though so doughty ever
in the rush of battle, shouldst thou risk abiding
the length of a night along with Grendel.'
    Beowulf spoke, the son of Ecgtheow:
530 'Lo, many things, my friend Unferth,
drunken with beer, thou hast said about Breca,
hast told of his journey! I will tell but the truth,
that I have more strength in swimming than others,
more endurance in hardness, more daring and power.
535 We two had boasted, boy-like and braggarts—
as yet, as I say, we were youths and not wise—
said one to the other that in the wide ocean
we would venture our lives, and verily did so.
When we entered the sound, a sword each had
540 to wield at his will, for we were minded
against whales to protect us. Nor in any wise could
        he
farther or faster in the flood go than I,
and I would not from him: we were companions.
Thus in the sea we swam together
545 five nights till the floods flung us apart,
the whelming waters and weather cold,
the darkness of night. The north wind came,
fiercely assailed us, and rough was the sea.
Ocean-bred monsters were angered with me;
550 against them, only my armor of mail
strongly made by man's hand helped me and saved
        me.

the interlocked corslet that lay on my breast,
brightened with gold. To the bottom bore me
my terrible foe, for he had me fast
555 in his direful grip, yet was granted to me
to pierce the monster with the point of my sword.
The storm of battle destroyed the sea-beast,
despite his power, through my prowess of hand.
So often and often my enemies
560 pressed me sorely. I served them well
with my faithful sword as was befitting.
They were baulked of the joy of a generous feast
when me they'd have eaten, those evil-doers,
sitting about in the depths of the sea.
565 So in the morning by me wounded,
along by the shore they lay cast up,
slain by the sword, and since then never
have they hindered or stayed the sailors faring
on the ocean deep. From the east came a light,
570 God's own bright signal, and the waves subsided,
so that I saw sea-nesses shining
and wind-swept cliffs. Wyrd often preserves
the hero undoomed if his valor endure!
To me it was given to get with my sword
575 nine of the monsters; and never heard I
of a harder night-battle under heaven's dome
nor of man more beset in the streams of the sea;
but worn with the struggle I saved my life
from the enemy's grasp. The ocean bore me
580 to the land of the Finns, the flood on its current,
the surging waves. Of such dire struggles
not a word has been told me concerning thee,
no exploits of battle, for neither Breca
in the throes of the fight, nor thou yet more,
585 has ever done such deeds of courage
with a bloody sword—nor boasting am I—

though thou of thy brothers wert the bane and the
    slayer,
of thy dearest kin. Damned shalt thou be,
in hell make thy payment, though thy head be so
    clever.
590 I tell thee forsooth, thou son of Ecglaf,
that never could Grendel such numberless horrors,
that monster dire, have done to thy chief,
such shame to Heorot, if thy heart were at all,
thy courage so strong as thou hast claimed.
595 But he has found that the feud holds for him
little to fear from thy folk and thee.
A vaunt without worth, that of Victory-Scyldings.
He seizes his toll and spares no man
of the tribe of the Danes, but takes at his will,
600 slaughters and slays, and from Spear-Danes expects
no vengeance to follow. But Geats, he shall find,
have courage and strength, as full soon I to him
shall witness in battle. He who wills may then go
without fear to the mead-hall, when the morning
    light
605 of the day succeeding shall dawn upon men,
when the radiant sun shall shine from the south!'
    Delighted then was the lord of treasure,
brave in battle; the Bright-Danes' prince,
the people's guardian, now gray-haired and old,
610 trusted Beowulf's help, having heard his resolve.
There was laughter heard, the heroes were clam-
    orous,
words were joyful. Wealhtheow entered,
Hrothgar's consort of courtesy mindful,
gold-ringed saluted the lords in the hall.
615 That best of women the beaker presented
at once, as was right, to the warden of East-Danes,
at the drinking of beer begged him be happy,
beloved of his folk. The feast and the hall-cup

he received with delight, illustrious king.
620 To each warrior and youth she went in due course,
the Helmings' lady, handing the flagon,
until came the time when in turn the queen,
adorned with rings, endowed with nobility,
offered to Beowulf the bowl of mead.
625 The prince of the Geats she greeted, thanked God
with wisdom of words that His will decreed
she might trust in the help of a hero at length
to settle their wrongs. He received the beaker,
the warrior fierce, at Wealhtheow's hands
630 and responded then, stirred to the battle.
Beowulf spoke, the son of Ecgtheow:
'When I embarked on the sea with my band of war-
          riors,
took my seat in the vessel, I resolved within me
to work without fail the will of your people
535 or to die in battle borne down in the grip
of my enemy's clasp. I shall accomplish
the feat of a warrior or find for my life
a hero's end here in this mead-hall!'
These words well pleased the woman's mind,
640 the boast of the Geat. Gold-adorned went she,
noble lady and queen, by her lord to sit.
    Then again as before were great words spoken
within the hall. Happy the people were,
eager, rejoicing, till his evening rest
645 the son of Healfdene would seek in due course.
He knew that a battle anon with the monster
was destined to come in the darkened hall
when the light of the sun should be seen no longer,
and the shadows of night, the shapes of the helmets
650 of blackness should gather, blindly advancing
and dim under heaven. The host all arose.
Then the king took leave of his lordly guest,
Hrothgar of Beowulf, and bade him succeed,

gave him rule of the wine-hall with words like these:
655 'To no man ever since of age I grew
to lift hand and shield have I left before
this noble hall save now to thee.
Have now and hold it, of houses most splendid;
be mindful of glory; thy might make known;
660 be on watch 'gainst the foe! No default of things
          wished for
shall be thine if the venture thou survivest with life.'
    Then out from the hall Hrothgar departed,
protector of Scyldings, to seek his queen,
the bed of Wealhtheow, with his band of retainers.
665 The King of Glory against Grendel had set
in the hall a warder, as is widely known.
He held to the task that was his alone,
from the monstrous foe defending the king.
The prince of the Geats in the pride of his strength
670 trusted loyally yet relied on the Lord.
He unburdened himself of the byrny of iron,
took the helm from his head, to a helpful thane
gave his sword richly chased, the choicest of weapons,
and bade him guard all the gear of battle.
675 Then great Beowulf of the Geatish line
with boastful words spoke ere he sank to his rest:
'I count myself nowise in the contests of war
feebler in vigor than my foe Grendel.
I will not therefore, though well I might,
680 take his life with my sword and slay him thus.
He has no weapons to hew my shield,
to strike against me, though strong he is
in deeds of hostility. We two to-night
will do without swords if he dare in battle
685 to engage with bare hands. Let God the omniscient,
the holy Lord the honor of victory
give to the one of us his wisdom decrees!'
The brave in battle then bent, and the pillow

was pressed by his cheek. The keen sea-farers
690 grouped about him bowed to their slumbers.
No one of them thought that thence he should go
to his dear home again, or again see his people,
the noble castle where nurtured he was;
for they knew that death had doomed too many
695 in the wine-hall before, not a few had destroyed
of the Danish folk. But the fortune of victory
the Lord had woven for the Wether people,
given help and support. By the power of one
should all overcome the enemy's craft,
700 by his might alone. Made manifest was it
that the God invincible governs forever
the doings of men.
                    Through the dark night gliding
came the shadow-goer. Asleep were the warriors
who were there to hold the horn-gabled hall—
705 but one was waking. Without the will of the Lord,
the men were sure that under the shadows
the demon enemy could never drag them;
but the vigilant leader the venture awaited,
sleepless and angry the issue of battle.
710 Then from the moors with their misty slopes
came Grendel forth with God's curse on him;
the ravager meant, of the men found there,
one to have as his prey in the high-built hall.
He made his way till, the wine-hall near,
715 the golden assembly of men he descried,
richly fashioned. Not the first time was it
he came to the home of Hrothgar the king;
but never before did he find such men,
so strong to grasp what fortune might give.
720 The joyless creature came creeping on
to the door of the hall. Though hasped with iron,
it withstood not long the strength of his hands.
He pushed wide open the portal then,

with anger stirred, and straightway entered.
725 Across the bright floor with a fury of heart
the monster shuffled, while there shone in his eyes
a horrid light most like to flame.
His furious glance fell on the warriors,
on the sleeping clansmen slumbering there,
730 the band of heroes, and his heart exulted.
The demon dreadful, ere day should come,
made sure of rending, wresting from all of them
life from the body, and likewise hoped
for a plentiful feast. His fate was other,
735 for he never tasted or touched a mortal
after that night.   Now the mighty
kinsman of Hygelac the contest waited,
the sudden attack of the treacherous enemy;
nor did the monster a moment delay,
740 but seized at once a sleeping warrior
in his forward rush, rent him unwary,
tore his body, drank the blood from his veins,
devoured him straightway. Of the victim soon
remained not a limb, for the monster had bolted
745 every whit of the corpse. Came he then nearer,
laid hands on the hero, whose heart failed not,
on the warrior at rest; he reached forth for him,
clutching and clawing; but the chief was ready,
rising up on his arm against the enemy's thrust.
750   Soon discovered the keeper of wickedness
there was not to be found on the face of the earth,
though the world were searched, a stronger man
of greater power in the grip of his hands.
He feared for his life, but found no escape;
755 to flee and to hide was his heart's one wish,
with his demon brood; he endured what before
had never come to him in the course of his days.
Then the hero remembered, Hygelac's kinsman,
his boast of the evening; up he stood,

760 held the monster fast, though his fingers cracked;
away pulled the giant; the warrior followed.
The enemy longed, if ever he might,
to loosen the grip and get away,
to flee to the fens. He felt the power
765 of his enemy's grasp. A grievous journey,
this that the monster to Heorot made!
    There was din in the hall; to the Danes every one,
to the dwellers at court, keen men and warriors,
terror it brought. Both were angry,
770 the duel furious. The dwelling resounded.
Great wonder it was that the wine-hall stood,
fell not to earth as the foes there fought,
but the beauteous house with bands of iron
within and without was everywhere strengthened
775 by skilful craft. Crashed there many
a gold-decked settle, the story says,
to the floor of the mead-hall while the foes were
              struggling.
The Scylding leaders had believed not before
that any man ever in any fashion
780 could damage that hall, adorned with antlers,
by wiles destroy it, save the whelming of flame
with fire should raze it. Rose up the tumult
ceaseless and dreadful; on the Danish folk
a terrible fear fell while they listened,
785 from without through the walls the wailing heard,
the cry terror-stricken that came from God's foe,
from the hell-bound wight, wounded, defeated,
the dire lamentation. He was tight in the grasp
of the hero mightiest of mortal men,
790 strongest of grip. The guardian of warriors
would in no wise leave alive the destroyer,
accounting him wholly an encumbrance to folk.
Round about Beowulf brandished his comrades
their ancient weapons, wished to protect

795 the life of their prince, their lord so glorious,
if they in any wise a way might find.
They were not aware when they went to the battle,
those warriors eager who entered the fray,
hacking and hewing with hearts that were bold,
300 seeking with iron the soul of the monster,
that him no weapon, no war-bill on earth,
though the choicest of swords, might cleave or harm;
for he had upon him the power of a spell,
an enchantment had woven that warded from him
805 the edge of them all. Yet his end was to be,
when the time of death came, the day of departure,
a miserable one, for the monster afar
in the power of demons was doomed to go.
    Now at length found he, who aforetime had
        wrought
810 much trouble for man and many afflictions—
God's enemy he, hostile and wicked—
that his body's force was failing and feeble
in the clutch of the hero, Hygelac's kinsman.
Each to the other was ever hateful
815 while life remained. The monster dire
was sorely hurt; his sinews gaped;
a wound on his shoulder was seen, and asunder
the joints were burst. To Beowulf victory
in battle was given, while Grendel sore-stricken
820 must flee away thence to the fens and the marshes,
to his home unhappy. He then clearly
knew that his days were numbered and spent,
that his life was ended. To all of the Danes
after the contest had come their desire.
825 The man from afar, faithful, courageous,
had cleansed the hall of Hrothgar and saved it
from the enemy's wrath. In the work of that night,
in the valorous deeds he had done he rejoiced.
The prince of the Geats his promise and boasting

830 had performed to the East-Danes; their ills and
    miseries
had ended at length, which inescapable
they before had suffered in sore distress
for no short time. The token was clear
when the proud in battle had placed the arm,
835 the shoulder of Grendel, and the hand he gripped
    with,
displayed them together under the gable.
    Then in the morning was many a warrior
about the hall, as I heard the tale;
from far and from near the folk-leaders came,
840 the wide ways over, the wonder to view,
the enemy's traces. Not at all did his death
seem a painful thing to the thanes who followed
the trail of the vanquished, tracking him down
where he went weary-hearted away from the hall,
845 smitten and dying, dragging his footsteps,
to plunge at last in the pool of the monsters.
Bubbles of blood broke on the surface,
the eddying swirls were swart with gore,
the crimson waters welled with his life-blood,
850 when he dove to his death. Doomed and joyless,
in the depths of the lake his life he gave up,
his heathen soul; then hell received him.
    High of heart thence, home again riding,
the old men proud from the pool of death
855 came on their steeds, and crowding youths
borne on their horses. Then Beowulf's glory
was often recounted; they caught up the tale
that between the two seas, southward or northward,
the wide world over no other man
860 under heaven's dome was doughtier ever,
among shield-warriors more worthy to rule;
yet in praise were disloyal to their lord in no manner,
to Hrothgar the gracious, for a good king was he.

Sometimes the brave in battle their horses,
865 their tawny mounts, when they met smooth paths,
sent racing forward as rivals in speed.
Sometimes the thanes who had songs in remem-
          brance,
famed for their minstrelsy, the men in whose minds
lived the old sagas, who could set them forth
870 woven rightly in words interlocked,
such men with skill made about Beowulf
chants of adventure, his voyage and battle,
aptly reciting the story all knew,
but in varying words. One recited
875 all the deeds he had heard of the hero Sigemund,
the many strange and mighty adventures,
the struggles and journeys of the son of Waels,
the battles known to none of the children
of men, and the feuds with Fitela's help;
880 such tales also as he told to his nephew
when they were together, for in the thick of battle
they were comrades ever, and often indeed
they slew with their swords the seed of the giants.
Fame not a little he found after death,
885 Sigemund mighty, the scion of nobles,
because the dragon that kept the hoard
he had slain with his hand. In the hoary rock
alone he adventured, nor was Fitela with him,
and alone the deed audacious accomplished,
890 for it came to pass that he pierced with his sword
the famous dragon and fixed in the wall
the marvellous blade. The monster was dead.
The demon by might had mastery gained
of the treasure he wished for and willed for his own.
895 This the son of Waels in a sea-boat loaded,
to the vessel's bosom bore the bright jewels,
while molten by its heat the monster perished.
Most widely vaunted of warriors was he

among the nations, by his mighty deeds
100 the throng's protector—and he throve thereby—
after Heremod's fame had faded away,
his strength and his power. By the people of Finn
betrayed was he into hostile hands
and swiftly slain. The surge of care
905 he escaped too long; a load of sorrow
was he to his nation and nobles all.
Yet in earlier days his exile's journey
many a wise man had mourned full often,
trusting his prowess from trouble to lead them
910 when the son of the prince with succor should come,
take the rank that was due him and rule the people,
the hoard and the city, the heroes' dominion,
the Scyldings' country. The kinsman of Hygelac
to all men grew more gracious and friendly,
915 while sin the heart of Heremod entered.
All this while the racers were riding their steeds
on the tawny lane. The light of morning
had hastened onward. To the high hall went
many a servant sturdy and valiant
920 to see the wonder. The warden of treasure,
the king himself from his consort's chamber
glorious issued with his group of retainers,
renowned for his virtues, and anon beside him
the queen with her maidens moved to the mead-hall
925 Hrothgar began—to the hall he had come,
looked from the step where he stood to the roof,
gold-adorned, lofty, and Grendel's hand:
'At the first, to the Lord let us be giving
our thanks for this sight! I have suffered much
930 from the hatred of Grendel. Yet God the glorious
may accomplish at will wonder after wonder.
But lately I hoped not while life should last
for my release, or relief from my sorrow,
while battle-gory the best of dwellings

935 stood wet with blood—a woe far-reaching
    to all of the council, since they could not hope
    the fortress to hold against hostile creatures,
    devilish monsters and demons of evil.
    But now has a champion accomplished for us,
940 through the mercy of God, the mighty deed
    which all of our wit, our wisdom and prowess,
    contrived not before. Lo, this may she say,
    whoever she be, the woman who bore him,
    if yet she lives, that the Lord her God
945 showed her His favor when such a son
    she brought into life. Now, Beowulf, thee,
    noblest of heroes, I heartily ask
    to be as my son; assume henceforth
    that kinship forever. While I hold rule,
950 no want shalt thou have of worldly possessions,
    since often for less to a lesser man
    have I honors granted, and given wealth
    to a feebler in deeds. Thou hast done such things
    that thy glory shall live to the last of the world,
955 forever and aye. May the all-wielding Lord,
    Who has guided thee hither, with good requite thee!'
        Beowulf spoke, the son of Ecgtheow:
    'Great mercy it was that we won the fight,
    the battle of strength, having boldly dared
960 the might of the foe. I had fondly hoped
    to show thee the corpse of the creature here
    as dight for the struggle but dead of his wounds.
    I had thought to hold him so hard in my grip,
    bind him so fast on the bed of death,
965 that he should there lie with his life as the forfeit,
    in agony bound till his body should fail.
    Though I would not loose him, the Lord did not
            grant
    that I should stay him or stop his going,
    my mortal foe; too mighty was he

370 in his power at the last. Yet he left his hand
   in saving his life, his shoulder and arm,
   nor was flight a help to the hapless creature
   in any wise, for the evil-doer
   is not destined to live the longer thereby,
975 pressed hard by his sins, for a sore wound has he,
   holding him close in its hateful grip,
   in its baleful clutch; abide he must there,
   foul with his sinning, the final doom
   when the Lord with justice shall judgment give.'
980   Now was silenced the son of Ecglaf
   nor boasted with pride of his prowess in war,
   while the nobles beheld the hand of the enemy
   by the hero's might on the high roof set,
   the monster's fingers. Before them each claw,
985 huge and horrible, of the heathen warrior,
   most like to steel each strong nail seemed.
   Every man was certain that a sword of battle,
   no matter how tempered, was not made with the
         power
   to pierce the demon or to pare away
990 the bloody clutch of his battling hand.
       Then by eager hands was Heorot decked;
   a throng there was of women and men
   who dressed the wine-hall, adorned for the guests.
   Golden-threaded the tapestries shone
995 the length of the walls, a wonder to see
   for all of the men who might behold them.
   Bright the house then and banded with iron,
   though all within was injured and broken,
   the joints of it rent; the roof alone
1000 was wholly sound when the hostile demon,
   stained with his crimes, despairing of life,
   fled in confusion. To flee is not easy—
   attempt it who will, and try as he may—
   since every mortal by the mandate of fate,

1005all the children of men, all the creatures of earth,
    must seek as appointed the place that is ready,
    where his body shall lie on its bed in the grave,
    asleep there forever.
                    Then into the hall
    at the hour befitting went Healfdene's son,
1010the king himself to sit at the feast.
    Never heard I of a nobler band
    with a greater pomp round a giver of treasure.
    There to the benches bowed the victors,
    rejoiced in the feast, fairly receiving
1015many a mead-cup; the kinsmen together
    sat strong-hearted in the towering hall,
    Hrothgar and Hrothulf. Heorot was peopled
    with friends on that day, nor deemed the Scyldings
    that treachery ever or treason should rend them.
1020A golden standard the son of Healfdene
    to Beowulf gave, a banner embroidered,
    with helmet and corslet and costly sword.
    In the view of the throng the victor's rewards
    were borne aloft. Beowulf emptied
1025a cup while standing. He could not with right
    feel shame of the gift in the sight of the warriors.
    I think that but few have four such treasures,
    adorned with gold, given to others
    in sign of their friendship while sitting at ale.
1030Around the helmet a rim projected,
    twisted with wire, to ward and preserve.
    No blade that the files for battle made ready
    could a warrior harm who bore to the contest
    a guard so fashioned against his foes.
1035The protector of heroes eight horses, then,
    with bridles plated, bade bring on the floor
    of the hall itself, and the saddle on one
    was wrought with art and rich with treasure;
    the seat it had been of the son of Healfdene

1040when the high king sought the sword-play of men.
Never failed in the van the valor of Hrothgar,
renowned for his courage when the corpses fell.
And the staff of the Ingwines bestowed as a gift
both of the treasures on Beowulf then,
1045the horses and weapons: they were his to enjoy.
Thus nobly the prince of power and fame,
the warden of heroes rewarded the struggle,
with treasures and steeds too splendid to scorn
by any man telling the truth as it is.
1050   Then to each of the men who made with Beowulf
the voyage on the sea the sovereign of warriors
bestowed a treasure as he stood by the mead-bench,
an heirloom gave he, and gold he promised
in guerdon of him whom Grendel before
1055had wickedly murdered—and more would have slain
if the God of Counsel and the courage of man
had not withheld him. All human kind
the Lord then governed as God doth still.
Always therefore are a thoughtful mind
1060and prudence wisest. Much weal and woe
must a man endure who days of struggle
in the life of the world long shall suffer.

There was song and rejoicing joined together
before the captain of hosts of Healfdene's band;
1065the harp was loud; a lay was chanted,
when Hrothgar's minstrel, merriment making,
related the story, as he stood by the mead-bench,
of the terror that seized on the sons of Finn.

The Half-Dane hero, Hnæf of the Scyldings,
1070was fated to fall in the Frisian battle,
nor could Hildeburh justly praise the Jutes' good
        faith.
Without sin of her own her son and her brother
she lost in the play of the lime-wood shields,
her dear ones who fell by their fate overcome

1075and wounded with spears. Sad was that lady!
The daughter of Hoc their death lamented,
with reason mourned when the morning came,
and under the sky the slaughter of kinsmen
she saw in the place so pleasant before
1080with the joy of the world. War had taken
the thanes of Finn save a few who were left,
and he could not fight on the field of battle,
struggle with Hengest or strike with destruction
in a war renewed the woeful remnant
1085of the thanes of the prince; but he proffered ʋ
treaty:—
that in another hall they should have their dwelling
with an equal share in the Eotens' rights,
the power over half of the hall and the throne,
and that Folcwalda's son freely should honor
1090each day in turn the Danes with Hengest,
distribute rings and bestow as much
in gifts of treasure and gold well wrought
to them as there came to the kin of the Frisians
when he cheered them with booty in the banqueting
hall.
1095Both parties then the pact confirmed
and made the truce fast. Finn to Hengest
declared with oaths of the uttermost power
that the heroes remaining should be held in honor
by the will of the counsellors, while no man in word
1100or in deed should venture to violate peace,
or ever mention with malicious heart
that by force of need they followed the prince
who had slain the lord of the leaderless band.
If any Frisian by an angry speech
1105should be reminded of the murderous enmity,
the edge of the sword should settle the matter.
Then a funeral pyre was prepared, and gold

from the hoard was brought. The best of the warriors
of the Army-Danes was dight for the burning.
1110The blood-stained sark could be seen on the pyre,
the gilded swine set on the helmet,
the iron-hard boar, and æthelings many
destroyed by their wounds—in the war they had
perished.
Then Hildeburh with Hnæf bade place
1115her son in the flames on the funeral pyre
to burn his body, on the bale-fire set it
by his uncle's shoulder. With songs the lady
lamented and mourned. Mounted the clamor.
Rose to the heavens and roared on the barrow
1120the huge death-fire; their heads were melted;
the blood sprang out when burst the gashes,
the wounds of their bodies. Whom war had
destroyed
the flame swallowed up, of spirits most greedy.
Departed the glory of the peoples both.
1125 Then the warriors dispersed and went to their
dwellings,
bereft of their friends, Friesland to see again,
their homes and high cities. Hengest unhappily
through the slaughter-marked winter awaited with
Finn.
He remembered his country, though he could not go
1130to drive on the sea a ship ring-prowed.
With storms the ocean surged and struggled
against the winds, while winter with ice-bonds
locked the sea-waves, until spring again
came to men's dwellings as comes it still,
1135wondrously brilliant, for the weather always
keeps to the seasons. Winter departed,
and the earth was fair. The exile guest
was eager to go, yet gave more thought

to his wish for revenge than a voyage on the sea,
1140 to plotting some means to meet with the Frisians
in hostile encounter, which held all his mind.
Thus he refused not to fulfil his part
when Hunlafing lent him the light of battles,
the best of blades in his bosom placed—
1145 its cutting-edge known to the nation of Eotens.
Again, too, death, cruel death by the sword
on bold Finn came and caught him at home
when Guthlaf and Oslaf at the end of their journey
bewailed with reproaches the woes that had come,
1150 the terrible onset, and tried not to bridle
their restless hearts. Then the hall was reddened
with the life-blood of foes, and Finn was slain,
the king with his courtiers, and his consort taken.
The Scylding warriors to their ships bore off
1155 whatever they found of Finn's possessions,
the gems and the necklaces, the jewels well-wrought
of the king of the land. The lady magnificent
they carried away when they went back to Denmark,
led to her people.

                The lay was finished,
1160 the song of the minstrel. Then mirth arose,
and loud grew the merriment when from lordly
        flagons
men poured out the wine. Wealhtheow entered
with a crown of gold on her head, and went where
        together sat
the uncle proud and the nephew, for as yet there was
        peace between them,
1165 trust of each in the other. Likewise Unferth the
        spokesman
sat at the feet of the Scyldings' lord, for his faith
        they trusted,
thinking his heart was noble. though in the heat of
        battle

he had proved disloyal to his kinsfolk. Then the
      Scyldings' lady spoke:
'Take this beaker, my treasure-king
1170and generous lord! May joy be thine,
  noble friend of warriors! Such words of favor
  as are fitting to guests to the Geats address.
  Be gracious to them and grant them gifts
  of the store thou hast found from far and from near
1175I am told that thou wouldst take for a son
  this hero of combats, since Heorot is cleansed,
  the ring-hall splendid. Then revel in gifts
  while life is thine, and leave to thy kinsmen
  thy fortune and realm when forth thou must go
1180to look upon death. I doubt not my Hrothulf
  of his grace to these youths will grant his favor
  if thou shalt leave, dear lord of the Scyldings,
  the world before him. He will, I feel sure,
  repay our care by the kindness he shows
1185to these sons of ours, ever remembering
  what we two of yore, while yet in his childhood,
  gave him of honors and of gifts desired.'
    Then she turned to the bench where her boys were
      sitting,
Hrethric and Hrothmund, with the heroes' sons,
1190a band of young men. There the mighty Geat
  Beowulf also with the brothers was placed.
  The cup she proffered with kindness to him,
  speaking in friendship; and spirals of gold
  were brought by her favor, two bracelets and rings
1195and a corslet, and more, the mightiest ever,
  as I think, of necklaces that was known on the earth.
  Under heaven's round I have heard of no better
  possession of heroes since Hama bore off
  to the city bright the Brosings' treasure,
1200the jewelled collar, escaped from Eormenric
  and chose the eternal, thus cheating his wiles.

This necklace, then, the nephew of Swerting,
Hygelac the Geat, had in possession
while the booty of battle under banner he guarded,
1205protecting his treasure. Overtaken by fate
was he when from pride a hostile attack
he made on the Frisians and found there sorrow.
O'er the cup of the sea he carried the jewel
wondrously precious, the prince in his power.
1210With his shield on he perished. To the power of
the Franks
the king's corpse and armor came with the necklace.
When the carnage was finished, inferior warriors
plundered the bodies, for the band of Geats
lay dead on the field.
                    Great din filled the hall.
1215Then Wealhtheow spoke these words before all:
'Take, dear Beowulf, as a token of fortune
this necklace, young comrade; this corslet enjoy.
They are precious treasures. So prosper well,
thy might reveal, and advice to these youths
1220give by thy kindness. I shall forget not requital.
The praise of warriors thou hast won for thyself
both near and far, both now and forever,
a fame as wide as the wind-swept walls
that the sea encircles. Be, sir, while thou livest,
1225happy and prosperous. I proffer thee freely
the gift of these treasures. Be good to my sons,
of thy deeds be gentle, and joy be thine!
Each warrior here truly is trustful of each,
to his lord is friendly and loyal of heart;
1230the thanes and the nation are united and ready,
the men-at-arms drunken. Do as I ask thee!'
    She went to her seat. Splendid the banquet,
the drinking of wine, for their destiny grim
the men did not know, nor what to many
1235was fated that night to befall when Hrothgar

went forth to his dwelling, the famous to rest.
The hall was kept by a crowd of warriors,
who guarded it now again as of yore.
They pushed back the benches and placed on the floor
1240 their beds and bolsters. Bowed to his slumber
one of the feasters who was fated to die.
They set at their heads their splendid shields,
protectors in battle; on the benches behind
the heroes rested their helmets tall,
1245 their corslets of mail, their mighty spears.
Their custom it was for war to be ready
not only when forth on forays they went
but also at home at every season,
to furnish swift aid when befell the need,
1250 the loyal clan to their liege lord dear.
Sank they to slumber. A certain one paid
for his sleep full heavily as happened before
while Grendel guarded the golden hall,
crimes committed, till came the end,
1255 death for his sinning. It was seen that night,
made clear to the stalwart, that still there lived
an avenger and foe the feud to maintain,
the grievous strife. Grendel's mother,
a female monster, remembered her grief
1260 in her watery den where she dwelt alone
in the cold, cold sea, after Cain long ago
his brother had slain, the son of his father.
Away into exile he went with his guilt,
marked with the murder from men had fled,
1265 dwelt in the waste-lands. Thence woke the monsters,
the spirits of woe, of whom one was Grendel,
the hateful outcast who at Heorot met
a hero who watched, waiting the struggle.
The monster seized him, but soon he found
1270 in the man a strength, a mighty power,
an abounding gift which God had bestowed,

for the Omnipotent Lord lent him His aid,
His solace and help. So he humbled the fiend,
overcame the demon, who to death went forth
1275abject, defeated, to the fen where he dwelt,
a foe of all men. But his mother now,
savage and ravenous, made ready to go
a sorrowful journey her son to avenge.

Came she to Heorot, where the hall was thronged
1280with sleeping Ring-Danes. Sudden and soon
the terror fell when the foe appeared,
the mother of Grendel, though greater the horror
he spread, as his might was a man's compared
with a woman's strength; like a warrior armed,
1285when his hammered blade with blood new stained
cleaves with its edge his enemy's helmet,
cuts through the boar-crest the bound sword keen.
Then they snatched in the hall their swords from the
      benches,
laid hands on their shields, but their helmets forgot,
1290gave no heed to their corslets, could not for terror
when the monster they saw. She was not staying,
but headed about in haste to be gone,
to save her life when she was discovered.
One of the heroes she hastily seized
1295fast in her talons, then turned to the fens.
Dearest to Hrothgar was he whom she slew
of all his retainers between the two seas,
a warrior mighty, a man of power.

Absent was Beowulf; after the banquet
1300another lodging had been allotted
to the famous Geat. A great cry rose
in Heorot then. The hand she had taken,
the blood-soaked trophe! A torture renewed
was this in the courts. The exchange was evil,
1305each party in turn paying a price
in the life of friends. Then the leader wise,

the hoary king, in heart was troubled
when he knew that no longer was living the thane,
knew that his dearest of vassals was dead.
1310Swift from his bower was Beowulf fetched,
the hero victorious. In the twilit dawn
the noble warrior, renowned among men,
went with his comrades where the wise king waited
if ever the Wielder of All would change
1315to a happier tale the tidings of woe.
Along the floor strode the stalwart hero
with his handful of friends; the hall re-echoed.
In words he addressed the wise among rulers,
the lord of the Ingwines, asked of the night-time,
1320if aught had been done to dim his content.

· Hrothgar answered, the helmet of Scyldings:
'Ask not of rejoicing! Anew comes sorrow
to the Danish folk. Dead is Æschere,
the elder brother of Yrmenlaf,
1325my counsellor wise and constant helper;
at my shoulder he stood in the shock of battle,
in the crash of the conflict, the clash when we
        charged
like the boars on our helmets. What is best in a
        warrior,
who seeks and achieves, such was Æschere!
1330He died in Heorot at the hand of a murderous
and wandering monster; whither she vanished,
content with her prey and proud of her killing,
I do not know. Thy deed of the night
before this she avenged, when in violent wise
1335thou didst Grendel slay by the strength of thy hands,
because he too long had killed my folk,
wasted and ravaged. He rests in death,
his life a forfeit; but forth came another,
a mighty slayer her son to avenge,
1340and far she has gone the feud in repaying,

as many a thane may think in his heart
who grieves for his ruler, the giver of rings—
woe hard to bear. The hand is gone
that was free to you all of all good things.

1345 'I have heard it said by inhabitants here,
who are people of mine and men of wisdom,
that they saw two monsters mighty and dreadful
haunting the borders and holding the moors,
creatures woeful. One had a semblance,

1350 in so far as by them its form was descried,
in shape to a woman, while its wretched fellow
in the likeness of man, though larger than others,
the waste-lands haunted. Him while living
my people knew by the name of Grendel.

1355 Not at all had they knowledge of any sire,
or whether before them were formed such demons
uncouth and strange. In a secret land
they keep to the wolf-slopes, the windy nesses,
the fearful fens, where the falling stream

1360 under darkening forelands sinks down in shadow,
a flood into earth. Not far is it hence
in the measure of miles to the murky pool,
over which bend trees bright with hoar-frost,
a wood well-rooted the water shadowing.

1365 There night by night may be noted a wonder,
a fire on the flood, and found can be no man
so wise among mortals who has measured the depth.
Though a hart be pressed hard, by the hounds over-
        run,
an antlered stag in search of cover

1370 after racing from far, he will rather give up
his life on the bank than leap therein,
or plunge in the pool. The place is uncanny!
The waves of it stirred by the stormy winds,
when the weather is evil, rise up to the clouds,

1375 heavy with darkness when the heavens are dark

and the sky sheds tears. On thee alone
is our sole reliance. Thou hast still to learn
that place of fear, to find if thou canst
the sinful creature. Seek if thou darest!
1380I will pay thee in treasure at a price unconsidered
to end the feud, as before I did,
in circles of gold, if again thou returnest.'
     Beowulf spoke, the son of Ecgtheow:
'Grieve not, wise man! Mourning is feeble;
1385it avails much more to avenge one's friend.
For each of us must the end abide
of our course in the world, accomplish what may be
of glory ere death; to the doughty warrior
after life has gone is left but fame.
1390Arise, let us go, guard of thy people,
to track this monster, the mother of Grendel.
I give thee assurance, escape she shall not
in the womb of earth, or wood on the mountain,
or ground of ocean, go where she will!
1395Have patience to suffer thy sorrows so many
for the space of one day. I deem that thou wilt.'
     Then the old king up leaped, to the Lord gave
          thanks,
to the mighty God, for the man's good speech.
Straightway for Hrothgar a horse was bridled,
1400a curly-maned steed. In state he rode forth,
the king with his band of brave shield-bearers.
Through the forest they strode till they found on the
          plain
the trail of the monster, the track she had made
as forward she marched o'er the murky moor,
1405bearing along the best of the men
who had watched with Hrothgar the home of the
          folk.
Dead was he, taken, his doom accomplished.
Thus over the steeps of the stony hill-slopes

went the son of nobles by narrow paths
1410 and lonely ways, a woeful region
of steep abysses, the abode of monsters.
Forward he went with a few of his men
whose skill he trusted to scan the place,
till he suddenly found dark fir trees leaning
1415 over a gray and ancient cliff—
a joyless wood. The water beneath
was gory and troubled. Grievous it was
to the Danish warriors, a woe of the heart
to the Scylding thanes, sad of endurance
1420 by all of the heroes when the head of Æschere
they found, as they gazed, at the foot of the cliff.
The waters were stirred and welled with blood;
a horn resounded with summons to battle;
the band of retainers on the bank sat down.
1425 They saw in the pool serpents swimming,
many sea-dragons of marvellous kind,
like the monsters which bask at the base of cliffs
and are seen in the mists of morning often,
braving all perils as they put out to sea.
1430 Away these beasts of the wild, these serpents,
rushed in their anger, roused by the tumult,
the sound of the war-horn. The warrior Geat
with his bow slew one in the waves where it swam,
for the keen arrow struck in the creature's heart;
1435 more slowly it swam in the swirling pool
as death came near; and now in the waves
was assailed by the barbs of boar-spears quickly,
hard pressed by its foes when its force was spent,
and dragged to the shore up the shelving slope,
1440 a monster wondrous. The warriors viewed it—
a terror strange.
                    For the struggle Beowulf
thrust on his armor nor gave thought for his life.
The broad-breasted corslet cunningly fashioned

and woven with skill in the sea would be tested,
1445to the hero's body be a protection,
　　that no hostile embrace might hurt his breast
　　nor his life be injured in the enemy's grasp.
　　The shining helmet to his head was a guard
　　and down in the depths, adorned with treasure,
1450was to plumb the sea and the surge of the waters,
　　a helmet encompassed with chains that a smith
　　had long ago wrought, with wonders fashioned,
　　with the figures of boars so bound that never
　　might the blade of a battle-sword bite through the
　　　　metal.
1455Nor the meanest of aids to his might was Hrunting,
　　the hilted sword that the spokesman of Hrothgar
　　had lent for his use. Not least was that
　　of the treasures of old; of iron was it,
　　stained with poison in stripes, and hardened
1460in the blood of battle. Who bore it in hand
　　found that it failed him in the battle never
　　when he joined in a venture, on a journey of danger
　　to the place of his foes. Not the first time this
　　it was set a daring deed to accomplish.
1465Though mighty of strength, remembered not truly
　　the son of Ecglaf what he said before
　　while drunken with wine. The weapon he lent
　　to a better warrior, forbearing to risk
　　his life, for he dared not endure the struggle
1470in the frothing waves. The fame he lost,
　　the glory of struggle. Not so with the other
　　when he had clad him in the clothing of war.
　　　　Beowulf spoke, the son of Ecgtheow:
　　'Famed son of Healfdene, hold in memory,
1475wise prince, now that I am prepared for the venture,
　　the loyal oaths, lord open-handed,
　　that thou hast uttered, if I at thy need
　　should sacrifice life, to stand to me ever

in a father's stead. To my followers be
1480the friend and protector if taken by death
I perish in battle, my companions' stay.
Likewise the treasures which thou hast given me,
Hrothgar beloved, to Hygelac send.
The lord of the Geats, when he looks on the treasure,
1485the son of Hrethel will see that I found
a generous giver of gold, and enjoyed
while I lived the rewards that my worth had brought
    me.
And let Unferth have the ancient heirloom,
the warrior famous his weapon splendid,
1490the sword of battle. Now shall I with Hrunting
do deeds of glory, or death shall take me.'
        After speaking these words, the Wether-Geat
            prince
would wait no answer, but went in haste;
in the surging pool plunged the warrior.
1495Though his might was great, it was many hours
ere he dove far down to the deep sea-floor.
Soon the greedy and savage creature,
who had held for half of a hundred years
the rule of the waters, became aware
1500that a mortal intruded on the monster's realm.
She clutched to seize him, but he clasped her firmly;
the hero's body was hurt in no wise
by the enemy's grip, for his armor was strong.
The mail withstood the strain of her fingers,
1505protected his life with its locked interweavings.
Then far in the depths, to her den the sea-wolf
bore the prince of rings. No power had he,
which angered him sorely, to swing his sword;
but many strange beasts, monsters of ocean,
1510pressed hard upon him, harassed him grievously.
With their tusks they threatened to tear his armor,
menaced the hero. Then the man perceived

he had entered what seemed the enemy's hall,
where no water could harm him, no hurt from the
flood,
1515since a roof gave protection from the rush of the
deep,
the fear of the sea. Then firelight saw he,
a gleaming blaze that brightened the dark.
It showed to the hero the sea-beast accursed,
the mighty water-wife. Amain he rushed
1520with his battle-sword, and stayed not his hand,
till the ringed blade sang on her scaly head
a fierce war-lay. But the light of battles,
as the creature found, failed the warrior,
the bright sword he wielded was weak against her,
1525could do no hurt, though it had endured
many a combat, cut through the corslets
and helms of the doomed. Now dimmed at last
was the pride in battle of the precious treasure.
Yet faltered not, nor failed in valor
1530the kinsman of Hygelac, for his heart craved glory.
The angry champion cast away quickly
his well-chased sword strong and steel-edged,
to the earth flung it, having faith in his strength,
in the might of his hand-grip. So a man must do
1535who desires to gain glory in battle:
be careless of life but cherish his fame.
The prince of the Geats was glad in the struggle;
manful in contest he caught by the shoulder
the mother of Grendel, gripped her so fiercely
1540in his furious onrush that she fell to the ground.
She recovered quickly and caught him in turn,
repaid the attack with a terrible onset.
Though the strongest of warriors, he with weariness
staggered
and crashed to the earth. The creature uncanny
1545pressed down upon him and drew her broad knife

with its shining edge her son to avenge,
her only born. But his armor woven,
a corslet linked, his life protected,
kept from entering sword-edge and sword-point.
1550Save for his armor, the son of Ecgtheow,
　　the prince of the Geats, would have gone his far
　　　　　journey
　　that day under ground. His doughty corslet
　　helped him and saved him; the holy Lord
　　the victory gave, for God the wise,
1555the Heavenly Counsellor decreed it thus.

　　He won to his feet, and the war-gear among
saw a victory-bringing blade gigantic,
a sword strong of edge, ancient, splendid,
a glory of warriors, of weapons the choicest.
1560So mighty it was that no man but he
could ever have wielded that work of giants
or borne into battle the beautiful sword.
The Scyldings' defender, fierce and enraged,
seized the chased hilt, swung the sword on high,
1565for his life was at stake; then struck with fury.
So strong was the blow that the bones of her neck
broke with the might of it; the blade pierced through
her fated body. On the floor she died.

　　The sword dripped gore; the swordsman rejoiced.
1570The gleam of the firelight filled all the cavern,
like the candle of heaven shining clear in the sky.
About the hall gazing, Hygelac's kinsman
turned to the wall with his weapon upraised,
　　grim and resolute gripped the strong sword.
1575The blade had not failed in his glory the warrior,
and now was his purpose to pay back to Grendel
the harm he had wrought to the West Dane folk,
the attacks he had made and the murders done
more often by far than only that once
1580when he had Hrothgar's hearth-companions

slain in their slumber and, sleeping fast,
devoured fifteen of the folk of the Danes,
and a band of like number had borne to his den,
a hideous prey. Him the champion
1585sternly requited when he saw at rest
the lifeless body of Grendel lying,
doomed in the struggle he suffered at Heorot,
dead in the cavern. His corpse sprang wide
as the sword-blade fell, for the stroke of the hero
1590was strong and hard; and the head he severed.
    Soon the warriors who waited above
and scanned with Hrothgar the shadowy pool
saw that the waters were welling and troubled
and reddened with blood. About the hero
1595the gray old men together were speaking.
They said that the noble would never return,
would never come back from the battle victorious
the mighty prince; and many were sure
that the wolf of the sea had slain him there.
1600Came the noon of day. The ness was forsaken
by the Scylding heroes; and homeward departed
the gold-friend of men. But the Geats stayed on,
though sick of heart, and stared at the mere.
They desired, but hoped not, to see again
1605their comrade and lord.
                    Then because of the blood
the battle-sword wasted, and a wonder came,
for the blade dissolved in shreds of iron,
melted wholly, as melts the ice
when the Father unwinds the fetters of frost,
1610the water-bonds loosens, Who wields all power
of times and seasons. In truth is He Lord!
Though he saw much wealth, the Wether-Geat prince
took from the cavern treasures but two:
the head of the monster and the hilt of the sword,
1615richly adorned. The damascened blade

had perished before in the fire of blood,
in the demon's venom, who had died in the cave.
Then he who in conflict had compassed the downfall
of his enemies swam, plunging up through the
  waters.
1620Cleansed was the pool, purified wholly,
since the demon uncanny his days had ended,
relinquishing the fleeting life of this world.
Came to the surface, swimming stout-hearted,
the guard of mariners glad in the sea-spoil,
1625the mighty burden he bore to land.
Giving thanks to God, his thanes went towards him;
the mighty clan in their chief rejoiced,
were glad when they saw him safe after battle.
Then from the hero were his helmet and corslet
1630speedily loosened. The lake grew quiet,
though still the water was stained with bright blood.
In mood exultant they marched from the shore,
the known path followed, went forth on their way.
Bold were the warriors who bore from the sea-cliff
1635the mighty head; heavy the burden;
no two, though sturdy, had strength sufficient
to carry it forth, but four were needed
to bring with labor, bound on a spear-shift,
to the golden hall the head of Grendel.
1640Forthwith to the hall, warlike and valiant,
the fourteen Geats together came.
Among them their prince, proud with his comrades,
was treading the plain on the path to the mead-hall.
Then entered at length the lord of the thanes,
1645the valorous man mighty in glory,
the hero high-praised, and Hrothgar greeted.
By its hair was borne in the head of Grendel
across the wide floor where the warriors feasted,
a terror indeed to the Danes and their queen,
1650a spectacle strange; they stared with dismay.

Beowulf spoke, the son of Ecgtheow:
'The gifts of the sea, O son of Healfdene,
lord of the Scyldings, which thou lookest upon,
we have brought as tokens to tell our glory.
1655Not easily did I endure the contest,
the undersea battle, but bore it by struggling
and survived with my life. A victim I should have
been
if God's protection had not given me aid.
I could not of Hrunting in the contest avail me,
1660in any wise use it, though the weapon be strong;
but the Ruler of Men by His mercy granted
—God who most often is a guide to the friendless—
that I saw on the wall a sword suspended,
beautiful, mighty, and the blade I seized.
1665When came the right chance in the conflict, I struck
the guards of the cavern. With the gush of their
blood,
hottest of battle-gore, the blade damascened
in my hand was melted. The hilt I took
from the foe by my prowess, having punished their
crimes,
1670as was right that I do, the death of the Danes.
My promise thou hadst that in Heorot thou
shouldst care-free slumber with thy company round,
nor fear the loss of the lives of thy people,
some in their prime, prince of the Scyldings,
1675and some in their youth, the thanes and the warriors,
the death of thy people as before thou didst.'
Then was given the golden hilt
to the aged warrior, the work of giants
to the gray-haired leader. It was left in the keeping
1680of the lord of the Danes, since the devils had fallen,
what was made by smiths of mighty power,
for the foe of God had gone from the world,
guilty of murder, and his mother also.

It came to the keeping of the king who on earth
1685was the best of those living along the two seas,
of those of the Danes who have dealt out treasure.
Then spoke Hrothgar. The hilt he gazed on,
the ancient relic with the record engraved
of far-off struggles. Then the flood destroyed,
1690the rise of the sea, the race of the giants,
slaying the wicked. Their works were strange
to the Lord Eternal; in the lap of the waters
the Ruler of All recompense gave them.
Thus on the sword-guard of shining gold
1695in the letters of runes aright it was graven,
set down and said who the sword so choice
had first wrought for himself with serpent adorn
        ment
and twisted hilt. Then Healfdene's son,
the leader spoke—and silent were all:
1700'The man who judges with justice and truth,
who remembers all among men from of old,
his country's guard, may call this warrior
one born to renown. Beowulf, famous
art thou, my friend, through far-stretching regions
1705among all peoples. Yet modest thou art,
being mighty but wise. As once we have vowed,
my friendship is loyal. A lasting consoler
thou shalt be to thy people, a prop to them ever,
a helper of men. Heremod was not
1710to the sons of Ecgwela, to the Scyldings what thou
        art.
He gave not joy but grievous slaughter,
destruction and death to the Danish people.
In his anger of heart he hewed down his comrades,
his table-companions, till he turned away,
1715that famous prince, from the pleasures of life.
Though above all men the mighty God
greatly exalted him and gave him support

in the height of his strength, yet the heart in his
     breast
grew thirsty for blood.   No thanks or rewards
1720he bestowed on the Danes for deeds of glory,
     but awaited with sorrow the suffering due him,
     eternal affliction.   Be taught by him therefore;
     perceive what is generous.   For thy good I have
          spoken,
     made wise by the years.   A wonder is it
1725how Mighty God to men distributes
     the gifts of wisdom through His greatness of heart,
     or a realm and a lordship: He rules over all.
     Sometimes in the love of his loyal kinsmen
     He lets the mind of a man repose,
1730in his native land allows him possession
     of a stronghold of warriors and worldly joy,
     puts under his rule an earthly dominion,
     a kingdom wide, till he cannot think
     in his folly of heart of his final end.
1735He continues prosperous, disturbed in no way
     by sickness or age, nor does sorrow darken
     his heart with its evil, nor enmity ever
     awake into war; but the world altogether
     fulfils his desires, and he finds no change
1740until pride beyond measure is the master of him,
     waxes and flourishes, while his warden sleeps,
     the guard of his soul; too soundly he slumbers,
     bound up in his cares, while comes the enemy
     and wickedly arrows of evil shoots.
1745Then the bitter shaft strikes in his bosom
     under his helmet, for he has no protection
     from the spiteful attack of the spirit accursed.
     His long-held possessions seem to him meagre;
     a miser he turns, and meanly no longer
1750splendid rings gives, but forgets and neglects
     the recompense owing for the honors granted him.

by the Ruler of Glory, by God of old time.
Then unevadable the end comes on him
when his fading body fails and dwindles.
1755He dies as is fated, and there follows another
who recklessly spends the riches he hoarded,
nor the treasure with care keeps in possession.
   'Valiant Beowulf, avoid such evils;
. best of warriors, a better course follow,
1760the counsels of heaven. Take no heed of pride,
O man renowned, since now is the time
of thy might and fame. It shall follow soon
that sword or sickness thy strength shall lessen,
or the grip of the fire, or the flash of the blade,
1765or the surging flood, or the flight of a spear,
or the burden of age, when the brightness of eyes
shall diminish and darken, and death, lord of men,
shall with sudden power have sway upon thee.
A hundred half-years under heaven have I
1770governed the Ring-Danes and given protection
in wars against many of the world's tribes in turn
by lance and by sword, till was left me none
I reckoned a foe under the round of the sky.
But a change there came for my country and me,
1775grief after pleasure, when Grendel appeared,
the ancient foe who found me out.
From his visits of enmity often repeated
great sorrow I bore. Thanks be to our God,
to the Lord Everlasting that in life I remain
1780now the conflict is ended, that my eyes may gaze
on the blood-stained head set here in my sight!
Go now to thy place. Take pleasure in feasting,
famous in battle. There shall be on the morrow
shared between us a rich store of treasure.'
1785   The Geat was happy, and hastened soon
to the wealth of the feast as the wise king bade him.
Then again as before fairly was lifted

the voice of rejoicing by the valiant warriors
who sat in the hall.   Night's helmet darkened
1790over king and companions.   The company rose;
the gray-haired king would go to his bed,
the Scylding lord, while a longing unmeasured
for sleep overcame the conqueror Geat.
The stranger prince was soon guided forth,
1795worn with adventure, by one of the thanes
who for courtesy's sake was assigned to attend
such needs as the chief and his clan should have,
the length of their stay, the sea-farers all.
The noble lord slumbered.   Spacious and gold-
adorned
1800the high hall rose, while rested the guest
till the gleaming raven in gladness of heart
gave news of the sun. Then soon on the shadows
daylight was waxing.   The warriors hastened,
for the clansmen were glad to go to their people;
1805the bold-hearted stranger would seek his ship,
on the journey afar was fain to depart.
Then the brave son of Ecglaf bade them bring to
him Hrunting,
prayed his acceptance of the precious sword,
and Beowulf gave for the gift his thanks,
1810said that he found it a good friend to a warrior,
mighty in battle, nor blamed he in words
the weapon's power.   A proud man he.
With their war-gear ready the warriors stood
eager to journey.   Up to the high seat
1815the noble leader beloved by the Danes,
the valiant hero, advanced to greet Hrothgar.
Beowulf spoke, son of Ecgtheow:
'We who fared on the sea, from afar came hither,
desire to say that seeking Hygelac
1820we purpose to go.   Good has been to us
thine entertainment.   Thou hast treated us well.

If ever on earth I in any wise may
earn by my merit more of thy friendship,
lord of warriors, than was won hitherto
1825 by deeds of conflict, I shall come to thee soon.
If I learn while across the circuit of waters
that the nations about annoy and menace thee
as thy foes in past days have done at times,
I will bring thousands of thanes to assist thee,
1830 warriors to help thee. For Hygelac, lord
of the Geats, I will answer, guard of thy people,
that though he is young in years he will help me
by words and by deeds well to honor thee
and bring to thee spears, strengthen, support thee
1835 when thou art in want of warriors' aid.
If Hrethric shall purpose, thy princely son,
to come at his will to the courts of the Geats,
he will find many friends. Afar to visit
excellent may be when a man is strong.'
1840 Hrothgar responded, speaking in answer:
'The Lord of wisdom these words has sent thee,
put this speech in thy heart. I have heard from no
man
so young a discourse more cunningly spoken.
Thou art mighty of power and prudent in heart;
1845 thy words are choice. I cherish the thought,
if it comes about that battle fierce,
that iron or sickness the son of Hrethel,
or the spear takes away that warden of peoples,
removes thy lord, and thy life is spared,
1850 that the Geats of the Sea a more suitable king
could not choose or a better to be the guardian
of treasure and heroes, if to hold thou desirest
the rule of thy kinsmen. The kind that thou art
pleases me, Beowulf, the better I know thee.
1855 Thou hast brought it to pass that peace shall be held
between our nations, the tribes of the Geats

and the Spear-Danes together.   Strife shall be quiet
and the hostile deeds they endured of yore;
and while I command my dominion wide,
1860our wealth shall be shared, and ships ring-prowed
shall bring many gifts o'er the gannet's bath,
often bring greetings over the ocean
and tokens of love.   I believe that the peoples
shall fast be united towards foe and towards friend,
1865blameless in all things in the elder fashion.'
    Then the son of Healfdene, helmet of warriors,
made gift of treasures twelve to the hero,
bade him seek in peace his people beloved,
but straightway return when time should avail.
1870Kissed him in parting the king high-born,
the prince of Scyldings his most precious of thanes,
and grasped his shoulders with the shedding of tears,
the gray-haired elder.   No expectation
had they of meeting once more in council,
1875he more than the other, whom age had made wise.
So dear was the man that he might not restrain
what rose in his breast; his blood was quickened
with longing deep-seated and love of the hero
who was bound in his heart by the bonds of affection.
1880Away turned Beowulf the warrior from him,
trod the greensward with gold resplendent,
with his treasure exultant.   At anchor riding
the sea-goer waited, the ship its master.
But still in going the gifts of Hrothgar
1885they often acclaimed; a king was he
blameless in all wise until age the destroyer
had snatched away his strength and his joy.
    Then came to the sea the company proud
of youthful warriors, wearing their corslets,
1890their woven armor.   The warder perceived
the return of the band from the tip of the headland
again as before, and greeted the strangers

with words of welcome when he went to meet them,
said that as friends, to the folk of the Wethers,
1895brave and bright-armored, they embarked on their
journey.
There beached on the sand was the ship ring-prowed,
a roomy vessel with riches laden,
with horses and armor. High above it
the mast overtowered the treasures of Hrothgar.
1900To the guard of the boat was given a sword
with a golden hilt, which gained him thereafter
in the mead-hall much honor for the heirloom he
owned,
for the treasure's sake. Then the ship to the sea
was launched, and went forth from the land of the
Danes.
1905 From the mast was spread a sail like a mantle,
made fast with cordage; there was creaking of
timbers;
not at all did the wind or the waves on the voyage
oppose the sailors. The ship went forth
with foam at its prow, floated seaward,
1910a craft well-caulked on the currents of ocean,
until they came to the cliffs of the Geats,
to the forelands they knew. Forward the vessel
by the wind was driven, and dashed to the shore.
The harbor warden, who had waited long
1915on watch by the sea for the warriors dear,
straightway perceived them from the strand where
he stood.
The craft wide-bosomed he bound to the sand,
made it fast by cables, lest the force of the waves
should sweep the fair ship seaward and crush it.
1920The æthelings' treasure, the trappings and gold,
he bade them bring forth; nor far was it thence
they must go to seek the giver of riches,

Hygelac Hrethling, at home where he dwelt
with his comrades about him, close to the sea-wall.
1925 The castle was splendid, the king most valiant;
the hall was lofty, Hygd very youthful,
wise and well-nurtured, though winters but few
the daughter of Hæreth had dwelt as yet
in the courtly limits. Not illiberal was she
1930nor mean in her gifts to the Geats, her people,
in the riches she granted. The radiant queen
had no heart like Thryth's with her horrible crimes,
for none dared brave that bold and fierce woman
of the honored courtiers save her own chosen lord.
1935If ever one gazed with his eyes upon her,
he found himself bound in the bonds of destruction
that hands had locked. Nor long did he wait
after his seizure till a sword adorned
with shadowed lines of his life made an end,
1940gave him the death-stroke. So to do is not queenly,
nor a lady's way, though lovely she be,
to take a man's life for a lie, pretending
an insult, since women ever should be weavers of
peace.
The kinsman of Hemming of this course made an
end.
1945Another tale has been told at ale-drinkings:
that fewer evils on the folk she brought,
deeds of wickedness after once, gold-adorned,
she was given as wife to a warrior young
of a high-born race, and the hall of Offa
1950o'er the tawny flood at her father's command
she went forth to seek. Thenceforward she dwelt
famed for virtue, and found on her throne
a life that was led by the laws of fate.
She held in high love the lord of warriors,
1955who of all mankind, as I have learned,
along the two seas was esteemed the best

of the sons of men.   Such was Offa,
a warrior brave and widely honored
for his gifts and his fighting, who gave wise rule
1960to the land.   Succeeded his son Eomer,
a help to heroes, Hemming's kinsman,
the nephew of Garmund, renowned in battle.
    Seeking Hygelac, the hero came marching
o'er the plain by the sea, o'er the sands with his com-
    rades,
1965the wide-spreading shore.   Shone the world's candle,
the sun risen high.   They hastened forward
till they reached the courts where the king, they
    knew,
the warriors' protector awaited their coming,
young and yet valiant, the victor of Ongentheow,
1970the giver of treasure.   They told to Hygelac
their tale of adventure, the voyage of Beowulf,
their chieftain in war, their comrade in battle,
who in safety had come as conqueror homeward,
surviving the struggle with strength unweakened.
1975Then quickly was made, as the mighty king bade,
a place in the hall for the heroes returning.
He who had come from the conflict greeted
with speech ceremonious and solemn words
his trusted lord.   He took his seat
1980by his kinsman's side.   With cups of mead
throughout the hall went Hæreth's daughter.
She praised the band and bore strong beakers
to the hands of the warriors.   Hygelac courteously,
eager and curious, his comrades questioned
1985in the lofty hall to learn what adventures
the Sea-Geats had found on their far-off journeyings.
'How went it with thee, well-beloved Beowulf,
when thou madest the sudden resolve to go
seeking battle across the salt water
1990afar in Heorot?   Did Hrothgar the famous

in any wise find thee an aid in his troubles,
which were widely bruited? I brooded thereon
with fervent sorrow, fearing the venture
for so precious a man; I prayed thee long
1995in no wise to meet the murderous spirit,
but to leave the South-Danes themselves their battle
to wage against Grendel. To God I give thanks
that safe and sound I see thee once more.'
Beowulf responded, the son of Ecgtheow:
2000'Few men have learned, my lord Hygelac,
of the mighty encounter when I met with Grendel,
what a struggle took place on the plain between us,
on the field where before had found many times
sorrow and misery unceasing ever
2005the Victory-Scyldings. I avenged all that,
nor may any kinsman on earth of Grendel,
no last survivor of the vicious tribe
bound in wickedness, ever boast of the clamor
he has raised at dawn. To the ring-hall came I
2010to give to Hrothgar my greetings at first.
Soon the famous son of Healfdene,
having tried my heart and tested my spirit,
assigned me a place by the side of his son.
The host was happy. Under heaven's vault
2015I have never seen more mirth after drinking
by men assembled. Sometimes most queenly
through the hall the peace-pledge of peoples went
round,
encouraged the youths, and costly rings
bestowed on the warriors ere she went to her seat.
2020Again through the hall came Hrothgar's daughter,
whom Freawaru by the folk was named,
bearing the ale-cup to each in turn,
from the studded beaker serving the heroes.
Youthful and gauded with golden jewels,
2025she is promised as wife to the proud son of Froda.

The guard of the realm, who rules the Scyldings,
has decided on this, considering prudently
that he may with the woman many blood feuds
and contests settle. Yet seldom anywhere
2030 will the murderous spear after monstrous slaughter
be left in peace, though lovely the women.
The prince of the Battle-Bards displeased may then
be,
and the thanes of the people for this, each one,
when he his lady shall lead to the hall—
2035 that sons of the Danes should be served by the band.
In their hands shall glisten the gleaming heirlooms,
the Battle-Bards' store of sturdy weapons,
when the ring-marked blades they brandish aloft,
until in the play of the perilous battle
2040 the lives of their comrades they lose and their own.
Then shall say at the beer-feast, when he sees the
ringed-hilt,
the warrior old who all remembers,
the death of the men, with a mind that is angered
trying the courage of his comrade young,
2045 in sadness waking to war's destruction
the thought of his heart, and thus he shall speak:
"Dost thou see, my friend, this sword and know it,
which thy father once to the fighting bore
in his final battle, this blade so precious?
2050 The Scyldings that day struck him down in his
helmet,
won the victory after Withergyld died,
when the heroes had fallen, the fiery Danes.
Yet now the son of a certain slayer,
exultant with treasure, is treading this floor,
2055 boasts of the murder and bears the possessions
which thou with right shouldst rule and control."
Thus time and again with grievous words
he shall urge and remind till the hour shall be

when the woman's thane by the thrust of a sword
2060 shall blood-stained die for the deeds of her father,
his life a forfeit. Afar shall the other
escape with his life, since the land he knows well.
Then the oaths once sworn on swords shall be broken
by each party of warriors, and shall pile up on Ingeld
2065 the waves of hostility. Towards his wife his love
shall cooler become for the care that besets him.
Thus I count not loyal the love of the Battle-Bards,
nor sincere the pact they plight with the Danes,
nor fast their friendship.

               'Now forth I shall speak
2070 of Grendel again, O giver of treasure,
that well thou mayst know how the war heroic
was joined and concluded. When the jewel of
      heaven
had passed over earth, the angry demon
dire and hostile in the darkness came,
2075 in the hall beset us where safe we were guards.
There the doom of battle and death assailed
the fated Handscio: he was first of the fallen,
the belted hero. He there by Grendel,
our famous comrade, was killed at a stroke,
2080 the body gulped down of our dear companion.
Nor yet away hence would the hideous slayer,
bent on destruction and bloody of jaw,
empty-handed go from the golden hall,
but trusting his strength he made trial of mine,
2085 with eager hand seized me. By his side there hung
a wide-mouthed sack of wonderful kind,
marvellously fastened and fashioned with skill
by the devil's craft from a dragon's skin.
The savage monster desired therein
2090 to plunge me, though guiltless against him was I,
one out of many. It was not to be,
for I stood upright in my wrath and faced him.

Too long is to tell how the terrible foe
I dealt with, avenging his victims each one.
2095 'The deeds I accomplished will be counted for
glory
to thy folk, my prince. He fled away then,
and thus saved his life for a little while,
yet his left hand behind him in Heorot stayed,
and he in misery, mournful of heart,
2100 went plunging down to the depths of the lake.
When the morning came and the company sat
together feasting, the friend of the Scyldings
gave me rich rewards for the work of the battle,
things massive of gold and many treasures.
2105 There was song and mirth; a Scylding ancient,
who much had learned, related past deeds.
Sometimes a warrior struck the wood of joy,
brought mirth with the harp, or a mournful song
and a true he sang; sometimes rightly
2110 the noble king told a tale of the best.
Sometimes again began the old warrior,
now burdened with years, of his youth to speak,
what strength had been his. His heart wise in
winters
was stirred with the memory of many things past.
2115 So we therein till the end of the day
made merry together, and to men returned
another night. Then anon the mother
of Grendel was ready to wreak her vengeance.
She journeyed sorrowful, for her son was killed
2120 by the hostile Wethers. The woman monstrous
avenged her son, slaying boldly
a man called Æschere, who was old and wise;
the counsellor's life was lost that night.
Nor might the Danes when the morning came
2125 on a flaming pyre place him for burning,
the man who was dear to them, by death overcome.

ın her hostile arms under the waterfall
she had borne away his body afar.
That deed was to Hrothgar the direst of sorrows
2130that the lord of the people had long endured.
Then the prince by thy life implored me, sorrowing,
that I in the welter of waters should show
my warlike valor, should venture my life,
should win new glory. Rewards he promised.
2135The watcher, then, as is widely known,
savage and terrible, of the sea-bottom found I.
With hands gripped fast we fought for awhile.
Blood heaved through the waters. The head I cut off
of Grendel's mother with my mighty sword
2140in the hall where we fought. My fate spared me
          yet;
she lost the struggle, and her life departed.
Then Healfdene's son, the shield of warriors,
gave me rich treasures again for reward.
    'Thus the king of the people in prosperity reigned;
2145nor did I fail to find my recompense,
the reward of my strength, for the son of Healfdene
gave me riches to the glut of desire,
which, king of heroes, in kindness I bring
to offer to thee. Thine is the favor
2150in which I must live. Relations save thee,
Hygelac, truly I have but few.'
    Then he bade them bring in the boar-crested
          helmet
that towered in battle, the byrny gray,
the splendid war-sword, and spoke thereafter:
2155'This equipment of war by the wise king Hrothgar
was given to me with the mandate that first
I should tell to thee the tale of its getting.
He said that King Heorogar had it of old,
the lord of the Scyldings for long possessed it.
2160Yet not to Heoroward, though he held him dear,

to his valiant son consented he
to give the armor. Be it all thine own!'
 Of treasures, I heard, four horses quickly
were shown thereafter, four steeds alike,
2165yellow-red like the apple. He offered them all,
the steeds and the riches. So is right for a kinsman,
and comrades should never fling the net of malice
over one another in ways that are hidden,
nor plot their death. Very dear was his nephew
2170to Hygelac, bold in battle ever,
and each remembered the other's benefits.
He presented, I heard, to Hygd a necklace,
a wondrous jewel that Wealhtheow gave him,
the prince's daughter, and proffered therewith
2175three horses saddled, supple and shining.
The ring she received and set on her bosom.
 Thus showed himself brave the son of Ecgtheow,
renowned in battle by his noble deeds.
He strove for glory, nor struck down drunken
2180his hearth-companions. His heart was not fierce,
though a gift magnificent God had granted him;
the mightiest strength among men he possessed,
a fighter loyal. Long was he wretched:
the sons of the Geats saw in him nothing,
2185and the lord of the Wethers little honor
set upon him when he sat on the mead-bench.
They greatly feared that feeble he was,
an ætheling slothful, yet to all his afflictions
an end was made for the man illustrious.
2190   Then the king brave in battle bade them bring to
     him,
the guardian of warriors, the gold-adorned
heirloom of Hrethel. Had not the Geats
a greater treasure in the guise of a sword.
This on the bosom of Beowulf laid he,
2195and gave him a hall, with hides seven thousand,

a princely seat. Ancestral rights
they held in common, the country's land
and the wealth of the nation; but one of them had
the wider rule, since his rank was higher.

2200 It came to pass in the course of the years
by the hap of battle that Hygelac died;
and the swords of war in spite of his phalanx
of shields brought death to doughty Heardred,
when warriors bold, the Battle-Swedes,

2205 sought till they found him, and sorely attacked him,
the nephews of Hereric with their hardy people.
Then to Beowulf the broad dominion
came as inheritance. He held it well
for fifty winters—as a warder old

2210 was the king of the land—till at length began
in the darkness of night a dragon to ravage,
who guarded a hoard on the heights of the heath,
a stone barrow lofty. There lay beneath it
a pathway unknown to the approach of men.

2215 A certain man entered, saw at close quarters
the heathen hoard, laid hands on a cup
that was richly adorned. The dragon discovered it,
though sleeping he was when the wily thief
played the trick on him. The people about,

2220 the folk of the nation soon found he was angry.
Not at all of his choice did he enter the dragon-
          hoard,
of his own desire, he who sorely wronged him.
A thane he was of the warriors' sons,
who fled in distress from his trials and scourgings,

2225 had need of a refuge and rested there,
the guilty man. A gruesome horror
to the sight of the stranger soon revealed itself,
and yet the miserable man was able
to escape the foe, since fated it was,

2230 when he had perceived the sudden terror.

The flagon he seized.   Many such there were,
ancient treasures, in the earthen house,
which some man had hidden whose heart was wise
in former years, the fortune enormous
2235of a noble race, the riches they cherished.
In days of old by death they were taken,
and he alone was left thereafter
longest remaining of the men of the nation,
lamented his friends and found no hope
2240that for more than a little he would live to enjoy
the ancient wealth.   By the waves of the sea
the mound stood ready, raised near the foreland,
newly built on the field, firm against trespass.
The guard of the rings his riches brought
2245and hoarded therein the hand-wrought gold,
the best of the wealth, and a few words spoke:
'Hold now, O earth, since heroes may not,
what warriors have owned!   Of old time from thee
valiant men took it.   Violence fearful,
2250death on the battle-field, has bowed them all;
all of my people have perished, renouncing
the joys of the hall.   I have not one left
to polish the flagon, the precious cup,
or high raise the sword.   The host has gone else-
        where.
2255From the helmet has fallen the fair-wrought gold,
the plates that adorned it; the polishers sleep
who once would have burnished the battle-mask.
So too the corslet that in combat awaited
the bite of the spears when the shields were crashing
2260has decayed with its master, for the mail of the byrny
follows not after when afar goes the chieftain,
by the warrior's side.   The sound of the harp
has gone with its merriment; no good hawk flies
the length of the hall, nor does fleet horse trample
2265the court of the castle.   The kinsmen all

have been scattered afar by the scourge of death.'
So in sadness of mood mourned and lamented
the one who was left, living unhappy
by day and by night until death's flood-tide
2270rose up to his heart. The hoard of joys
was found standing open by the foe of darkness,
the naked dragon who night by night,
encircled with fire, aflame sought the cliffs,
flew doing evil. The earth-dwellers held him
2275in exceeding dread. He was destined to find
the hoard in the earth, and the heathen gold
he kept through the years though it yielded no profit.
For three hundred winters the worker of evil
held possession of the hoard in the earth,
2280the treasure enormous, until he was angered
by the man who bore a beaker adorned
to the lord he served, seeking from him
peace and forgiveness. They explored the treasure,
they took away rings, to the wretched man
2285they allowed what he sought. The lord then first
saw what had been made by the men of old.
But the serpent awoke with wrath renewed;
he nosed at the stones and stout-hearted found
the track of his foe. Forward stealthily
2290towards the head of the monster moved the enemy.
A man may well through woe and misery
pass if unfated and the favor has gained
of the Ruler of All. The eager guardian
went circling the place in search of the man
2295who during his sleep had sorely tricked him.
Enraged and furious he ranged about often
the barrow's circuit, but by it no man
was there on the heath. He was hot for the conflict,
for the time of action. He returned to the barrow,
2300sought for the flagon, but soon he made sure
that some man had tampered with the treasure there,

had rifled the gold. The guardian waited
uneasy, impatient, until evening came.
Then the barrow's warder boiled with anger.
2305 The foe would avenge with fiery flame
the theft of the cup. When came day's end,
which the dragon had waited, on the wall he stayed
        not,
but soon departed encircled with flame
and trailing hot fire. To the folk of the land
2310 the beginning was awesome and the ending grievous
that swept on their lord with swift destruction.
   Then the sprite began to spew out fire.
The gleam, as they burned, from the glorious courts
was a horror to men. The hostile cloud-flyer
2315 alive in the dwellings would leave not one.
The dragon's warfare was widely seen,
his enmity known both near and afar,
how the destroyer harried the Geat folk,
humbled the people. He hastened back
2320 ere dawn to his treasure-hall, to the hoard he
        guarded.
The land he had circled with the light of his flame,
with destruction and burning. In his barrow he
        trusted,
the home whence he ravaged, but his hope deceived
        him.
   Straightway the terror was told to Beowulf,
2325 made known in truth, that the noblest of dwellings,
his home had crumbled in the clutch of the fire,
the throne of the Geats. Great and dire woe
the good king suffered, sorrow of heart.
In his wisdom he deemed he had deeply angered
2330 the Ruler Eternal, Whose right is of old,
the Lord Everlasting. There leapt dark thoughts
in his surging breast, which was steady before.
The fortress of peoples had the fire-dragon

destroyed with its flames, the stronghold wasted,
2335the land by the sea. The lord of the Wethers,
the war-king devised vengeance therefor.
He bade them make a marvellous shield
all of iron, the aid and protector
of nobles and warriors, for he knew right well
2340that a shield of linden could shelter him not,
wood against flame. He would wait the end
of his mortal days; but the dragon, too,
should finish its life with the lord of the people,
though long it had held its hoard of treasure.
2345Too proud was the king, the prince long famed,
the far-flying monster to fight with his band,
with an army in force. He feared not the contest,
nor dreaded at all the dragon's power,
its strength and its might; for struggles many
2350he had braved and endured, daring adventure
in the crash of battle, since he cleansed by his deed
the hall of Hrothgar and, hailed as a victor,
in his grip of death crushed Grendel's kin,
the hateful race.
Of his hand-to-hand battles
2355not the least was that when lost was Hygelac,
when the king of the Geats in the combat of war,
the lord of the folk in Friesland perished,
when the son of Hrethel was struck by a sword
in a bloody battle. Thence Beowulf came
2360by his strength alone, by swimming escaped.
The war-gear of thirty was thrust on his arm
when he plunged in the sea. Of the play of the
weapons
when on foot they struggled before, and against him
carried their linden-woods, no cause had the Hetwares
2365to be exultant. From the battle came few
of the warriors home. Through the waters' expanse,

lonely and sorrowing, the son of Ecgtheow
with grieved heart swam again to his people.
There Hygd offered him the throne and its riches,
2370treasure and sovereignty, her son mistrusting
as too feeble to hold, with Hygelac dead,
the seat of his fathers against foreign tribes.
Yet though they were miserable, they moved him not,
could persuade the noble in no wise to take
2375the lordship from Heardred, his liege to be,
or to rule for himself with royal power.
By friendly counsel he cared for him always,
with honor and favor until older he grew
and governed the Wethers.

                       Him woeful exiles
2380o'er the sea came seeking, the sons of Ohtere.
They cast off allegiance to the lord of the Scylfings,
had rebels become to the king of the sea,
of those who held sway in Sweden the strongest,
a famous prince. He found his death in it,
2385the son of Hygelac: for receiving them there,
by the blow of a sword he was slain and destroyed.
After Heardred perished, departed forthwith
the son of Ongentheow to seek his home.
He left the rule of the realm to Beowulf,
2390to govern the Geats: a good king he.
For that terrible woe he took his vengeance
in later days; to destitute Eadgils
became a friend when in force he advanced
across the wide sea, the son of Ohtere,
2395with embattled weapons and wrought his revenge
in a fierce attack, took the king's life.

    Through every trouble and terrible conflict
the son of Ecgtheow had safely passed,
through deeds of valor, till the day came on
2400when he must do battle with the hideous dragon.
In the fury of anger with other twelve

went the lord of the Geats to look on the dragon.
He had found ere this how the feud had begun,
the mortal enmity, for the man who had seized
2405 the precious beaker had brought it to him.
The thirteenth was he of the troop of warriors,
who had caused by his deeds the conflict and strife.
On their way they were led by the woeful captive
with gloom in his heart, a guide though unwilling,
2410 since he alone knew where near to the sea
the hill was placed, the hall under earth
by the surge of the ocean. Within it was full
of wealth magnificent. The warrior monstrous
was guarding still the gold of his treasure
2415 in the cave as of old. No easy adventure
for any man was it to enter the cavern.
On the headland he sat, and his hearth-companions
saluted once more the mighty king,
the lord of the Geats, with grave hearts and sad.
2420 For the fray he was eager, though Fate was near
and was soon to greet the gracious old man,
seek the soul within him and sunder apart
his life from his body. Not long was his spirit
to remain enclosed in the clothing of flesh.
2425 Beowulf spoke, the son of Ecgtheow:
'Many things I endured in the days of my youth,
wars and combats. I recall them all now.
The lord of the tribes, the treasure-prince took me,
from my father received me in my seventh winter,
2430 held me and kept me, Hrethel the king;
with feasting and treasure in his friendship was constant.
As long as he lived no less I was to him
in the courts where I served than the sons that were
his,
Herebeald, Hæthcyn, and my Hygelac dear.
2435 To the eldest came death by the deed of his brother,

by a chance unfitting was the fatal couch spread,
when Hæthcyn him with the horn-bow slew,
struck down his kinsman with the shot of an arrow
when he missed his mark and murdered his lord,
2440 one brother the other with a bloody dart.
  There could be no atonement for that terrible sin
which wearied the heart. A horror it was
that the ætheling's life should be lost unavenged.
  'Sad is it also for an aged man,
2445 hard to suffer, when his son rides high,
young on the gallows. With grief he laments
in a song of mourning for the son who hangs there
as food for the raven; and he finds no help,
though old and wise no aid can give him.
2450 Always at morning he remembers his sorrow,
that the youth has gone. He gives no heed
to another heir, another desires not
to see in his castle, since has come to his end
the one who was dear by death's strong hand.
2455 With sorrow he sees his son's habitation,
the wine-hall waste, the wind-swept chamber
whence pleasure has gone. In the grave are the
      horsemen;
the heroes slumber; no harp resounds;
in the courts no longer is laughter upraised.
2460 Then he goes to his chamber; again he laments,
continually sorrows. Too spacious the dwellings,
too wide are the plains.
                    'Thus the Wethers' ruler
mourned for Herebeald, and his heart was sore,
weighted with trouble. No way was there ever
2465 to punish the slayer and settle the feud.
He could find no means on the man to take ven-
      geance
for the loathly deed, though he loved him no more.
Thus sorely oppressed with sorrow too great

he gave up life's joy and God's light attained.
2470He left to his sons his land and his castle
  when he went from life, as must woeful and happy.
    'Then strife and enmity between Swedes and Geats
  across the broad sea broke into violence
  and fighting hard after Hrethel died,
2475for the heirs were bold of Ongentheow,
  warriors eager, and would not keep
  the peace overseas, but savage raids
  on Hreosna mound they made full often.
  My kinsmen and friends with fury took vengeance
2480in battles renewed, as is known to all,
  though one of them paid with a price therefor,
  a heavy cost, since Hæthcyn was slain,
  the lord of the Geats there lost his life.
  Then my other kinsman by the edge of the sword
2485avenged his murder one morning, I heard,
  in the duel of Eofor with Ongentheow.
  His war-helm split: the Scylfing aged
  was felled by a hand that full well remembered
  his hostile deeds and withheld not the stroke.
2490 'I repaid in warfare the wealth that Hygelac
  bestowed upon me, repaid what he gave me
  by my shining sword. He settled upon me
  lands and a dwelling, a delightful home;
  not needed he ever thereafter to seek
2495among Gifths or Spear-Danes or in Sweden a
      warrior
  of lesser power, for a price make him his.
  In the van of the host I held my place.
  Alone was I always, and ever shall lead
  in the struggle of combat while this sword shall
      endure,
2500which has served me often both early and late
  since I slew with my hand, when the host was as-
      sembled,

Dægrefn the warrior, the doughty Frank.
He could bring in no wise my breast adornments,
the arms I carried, to the king of the Frisians,
2505but bearing the standard on the battlefield died
the ætheling strong; nor was slain by a sword,
since the grip of my hands his heart-beats stopped,
his body destroyed. But the blade's edge now,
my hand and my sword, for the hoard shall battle.'
2510 For the last time Beowulf with brave words spoke:
'Many deeds of war I dared in my youth;
and once more still in the wisdom of age
as the guard of my people I will go to the conflict,
will add to my glory, if the evil creature
2515shall seek me out from its earth-hidden hall.'
Then greeted he the helmeted warriors,
each loyal man in a last farewell,
his comrades dear: 'I would carry no sword
against the dragon, nor deign with a weapon
2520to meet the monster if I might in some wise
proudly grapple, as with Grendel I did;
but I deem that its breath is deadly and hot,
a venomous flame. I shall venture, therefore,
with corslet and shield. Not the space of a foot
2525will I give by the cliff to the guard of the cavern,
but there shall await what Wyrd may decree,
the Lord of mankind. With courage of heart,
but making no boast, I shall meet the dragon.
Abide near the cave, ye bold men in corslets,
2530armed with your war-gear, and wait there the outcome,
which one of us twain shall win in the contest,
come forth as the victor. The venture is mine,
for no other man has might sufficient
or measure of power the monster to fight—
2535the deed of a warrior. I shall win the gold

by boldness and strength or in battle shall perish;
and dreadful shall be the death of your lord.'
   With helmet and shield, the hero bold
arose and went forth, firm in his courage,
2540 to the mouth of the cave. No coward's adventure!
He trusted the strength of his stalwart arm.
Endured had he much in the day of battle,
the crash of arms, the clashing of standards.
His courage was steadfast. Then he saw in the cliff
2545 an archway of stone, and out there issued
a stream from the cavern, the surge of it hot
with death-dealing fires. In the depth of the rock
could no man remain for a moment's space
alive and unburnt by the breath of the dragon.
2550 Stirred with fury, the stout-hearted Geat
let words from his bosom break in his anger,
shouted defiance. Resounding and clear,
his voice was heard in the hollowed rock,
and roused the warder, for its wrath was kindled
2555 that a man came near. No more was there time
to ask for a truce. Out from the cavern
the breath of the fiend came forth in a flood,
a venomous reek. The rock resounded.
Against the monster the man made ready
2560 his shield as a guard, the Geats' dear lord.
   Then was the rage of the ring-dragon stirred
to enter the conflict, while the king of battles
drew out his sword, the ancient heirloom,
his bold-flashing weapon. Both felt terror,
2565 each of the other, as their enmity stirred.
Behind his tall shield with stout heart waited
the lord of his clansmen, while quickly the dragon
coiled for the onset; in his corslet he waited.
Then breathing out fire, to its fate the monster
2570 came snakily gliding. The glorious prince
not long was protected in life and in body

by the shield he carried. He could not tell,
and his mind sought to fathom, why fate had not
         granted
for the first of all times triumph in battle.
2575He lifted his hand, the lord of the Geats,
and struck the dragon dreadful in motley
with his ancient blade. Though bright the edge of it,
it bit but feebly on the bone, and failed,
when its master had need, by the monster hard
         pressed.
2580Then savage of mood at the stroke of the weapon,
the guard of the barrow belched out its venom
in deadly flame; the fires spread wide.
   No joy of victory had the generous prince
of the folk of the Geats; failed him in battle
2585had his unsheathed sword, the iron he trusted,
his faithful weapon. For the famous king
hard was the voyage, the venture new,
hard the departure from the plains of the world
for a dwelling elsewhere, as each man must go
2590when his fleeting days are finished here,
though his will be to stay. They waited little,
the combatants fierce, but the contest renewed.
The treasure guardian again took heart
and breathed forth flame; with fire surrounded
2595the hard-pressed lord who had long borne rule.
No longer stood comrades in a company round him,
warriors noble, known for their valor.
They had fled in terror to the forest far off
to save their lives. But sorrow of heart
2600filled the mind of one, for may not forget
what to kinship is due the clansman loyal.
   The man was called Wiglaf, Weoxstan's son,
a shield-warrior keen and kinsman of Ælfhere,
of the Scylfing stock. He saw that his lord,
2605despite his helmet, by the heat was oppressed.

He remembered the honor the other had paid him,
the wealth and estate of the Wægmund line,
all the folk-rights that his father possessed.
He could not forbear; his buckler he seized,
2610his yellow shield; his sword he drew,
ancient and famous, the heirloom of Eanmund,
the son of Ohtere, who was slain in battle
friendless, an exile, by the arm of Weoxstan,
by the slash of his blade. He bore to his kinsman
2615the glittering helmet, the gleaming byrny,
the giant's sword old, but Onela spurned
the trappings of war worn by his nephew,
the still useful gear. He spoke not of vengeance,
though his brother's son had been slain by Weoxstan,
2620who kept for long the corslet and sword,
saved the treasures till his son was of age
to perform deeds of valor like his father before him.
He gave him the war-gear amongst the Geats where
   they dwelt,
left it all freely when from life he departed,
2625went forth in his age. The first time it was
that the champion young with his chieftain and lord
had come into battle; but his courage of heart
was steadfast in danger, and the sword of his sires
did not weaken in combat, as the war-dragon found
2630when they met together. Much that was truthful,
many words that were just, Wiglaf uttered,
as he spoke to his comrades in sadness of heart.
'I remember the time when mead we were drinking
and he gave us these bracelets in the banquet hall,
2635these helmets, these swords hardened and tempered;
we promised our lord we would pay him at need
for the trappings of war if a time should come
like this now upon us. Therefore he took us
himself from the army, holding us worthy
2640of adventure and glory, gave us these treasures,

because he accounted us chosen warriors,
courageous and loyal, though our lord intended
alone to accomplish this combat of strength
as guard of his folk, since glorious deeds
2645he was fain to perform, was the first of all men
in reckless daring. Now the day is come
when our lord requires the loyal strength
of valorous warriors. Let us venture and go,
give help to our chief, since here in the terror
2650of flame he has need. God knows that to me
it seems far better that my body perish
with the giver of gold engulfed by the fire.
It would ill become us to enter the court
still bearing our shields, save as preservers
2655of the life of our prince, the lord of the Wethers,
having vanquished his foe. For verily he
has better deserved than to battle alone,
to fall in the combat, affliction to suffer
bereft of comrades. Corslets and helmets,
2660our swords and our mail, must be shared by us all.'
    Through the deadly reek he rushed in his helmet
to the aid of his lord, while he eagerly spoke:
'Beowulf beloved, thy boast accomplish
which was uttered in youth when thy years were
few,
2665that never while living thou wouldst let thy glory
crumble and fall. In defence of thy life
show thy full power, prince strong-hearted;
be steadfast in courage. I come to thy aid!'
When he had spoken, came a second time
2670the enemy dire, the dragon enraged,
attacking with waves of terrible fire
the men it hated. In the heat of the flames
his shield with its boss was burned, while his corslet
was useless to aid the youthful warrior,
2675but the shield of his kinsman gave shelter to him

when his own was devoured in the vomit of flame.
　　Then the king once more, the mighty in battle,
remembered his glory, with main strength struck,
wielded with fury his war-blade Nægling,
2680and drove it home in the head of the dragon.
　　But shivered and failed the sword of Beowulf,
the gray and ancient.　His gift it was not
that blades of iron might ever in battle
help him to conquer.　His hand was too strong,
2685the strain too great when he struck, I am told,
for any weapon he wielded in combat,
though wondrously tempered; nor well was it for
　　him.
　　Then a third time advanced the violent foe,
the furious dragon in a fiery charge;
2690rushed on the chieftain when its chance had come
with a fierce attack, and fastened its jaws
in the neck of Beowulf, whose blood with his life
poured out from the wound in waves of gore.
In the king's distress his comrade in arms
2695showed forth his courage by a feat of might,
with the boldness and strength that were bred in
　　his line.
He took no heed of the head of the dragon,
but the bold man's hand was burned when he struck
a little below in his lord's defence
2700and drove his sword so deep in the monster,
his fine-wrought blade, that the fire thereafter
began to lessen.　Then the king of the Geats,
with his senses returned, seized the battle-knife
that hung on his corslet, a keen-edged blade,
2705and split the dragon with his stroke asunder.
　　They had slain the foe, slain it with valor,
shared in the enemy's end and destruction,
the kinsmen noble!　At need should be
all thanes like Wiglaf.　But this for the prince

2710was the last of victories, the latest of deeds,
of his works in the world. For the wound that
before
the earth-dragon gave him began now at length
to burn and to swell, and soon he found
that the venom within him with violent rage
2715rose up in his breast. The bravest of heroes,
the wise-hearted warrior, by the wall sank down
and leaned against it. He looked on the work
of giants about him, the great stone arches
and the columns supporting the cave immemorial.
2720Then the loyal thane laved with water
his chieftain and friend, the famous prince
bloody and wounded, worn with the battle,
with his hand he laved him, and his helmet un-
fastened.
Now Beowulf spoke despite his hurt,
2725the wound that was mortal, for well he knew
that his days were ended, that done was he
with the joy of earth, that all the tale
of his days was spent—and death most near:
'Now I to my heir, had any been granted me,
2730to the son of my body, had son been given,
to wear it hereafter my armor of war
would here bequeath. I have held this people
for fifty winters; no folk had a king
of the neighbors about us, none had a leader
2735who dared undertake an attack upon me
with swords and warriors. I waited unmoved
the judgments of fate, with justice ruled,
never sought to win by the wiles of war,
nor swore false oaths. Now stricken with wounds,
2740with death nigh at hand I am happy in this,
that the Lord of men need lay at my charge
no slaying of kinsmen when I come to depart
and leave my body. Now boldly go,

Wiglaf beloved, and look at the hoard
2745in the cavern gray, since the guardian lies
asleep from its wounds, despoiled of its treasure.
Make haste that I may behold the wealth,
view well the gold and the gems in their radiance,
and so beholding, for the sake of the treasure
2750more peacefully go, giving then over
my life and my lordship, which long I have held.'
The son of Weoxstan the speech of his lord
who was wounded in battle obeyed then quickly;
wearing his corslet of woven mail,
2755of intertwined rings, he entered the cave.
There the young thane perceived, and seeing exulted,
as he passed by the seat, a great pile of jewels,
on the earth the glitter of gold wide-scattered,
and the walls of the cavern a wonder to see,
2760for cups adorned the den of the dragon,
vessels once shining but now shorn of their beauty,
from the days of old. No dearth was of helmets
ancient and rusted, arm-bands aplenty
cunningly twisted. For treasures of gold,
2765when buried in earth, may easily last
far longer than he who hid them therein.
And a banner he saw shining all golden,
hanging high o'er the hoard, of handiwork marvellous,
skilfully woven. He scanned by its radiance,
2770so wondrous the light of it, the walls with the
treasure
and the floor of the cave; but he found of the
dragon
no sign at all, for the sword had destroyed it.
Thus a single man, they say, in the cavern
plundered the treasure of plates and cups,
2775till his arms were laden with the old work of giants;
and the banner, too, brightest of standards,

he brought forth with him. The blade of the hero,
the iron sword, had slain already
the monstrous guard which for many a year
2780 had kept the hoard by the heat of flame,
which filled with terror and the fires of death
the darkness of night while the dragon lived.
  The brave envoy hastened, eager to show
the wealth he had brought and wondering much
2785 if he still should find where before he had left him
the prince of the Wethers with wounds that were
  mortal,
his lord still living. Laden with treasure,
he came to the famous king and found him
spent and bloody, expiring, it seemed,
2790 with life at an end. But at length when water
he had cast upon him, the king began
in words that broke from his breast in sorrow
to speak, as the gold he saw before him:
'For all these riches to the Ruler Almighty,
2795 to the King of Glory I give my thanks,
to the Lord Eternal, that I leave such wealth,
may have ere I die what here I see
to bestow on my people. The price I have paid
is my ripened years; they are reaped for the treasure.
2800 Hold them in keeping, since the hoard is so bought,
the care of the tribesmen. I can no longer.
Let the warriors famous, when the fire consumes me.
build on the foreland a barrow splendid,
which shall keep me in memory among my people,
2805 as it rises high on the headland Hronesness;
and sea-farers ever, seeing, shall call it
Beowulf's barrow, when the ships high-built
through the mists of ocean come sailing from far.'
  Then took the brave prince from his throat a
  necklace,
2810 a golden collar, and gave the young warrior

his gold-decked helm from his head and his ring,
his corslet gave him, bade keep them well.
'Last remaining thou art left of our kinsmen,
of the Wægmund tribe, for Wyrd has swept
2815 away my clansmen, the warriors valorous,
all to destruction; and I must follow.'
For the last time thus the thoughts of his heart
the old king uttered, ere he came to the pyre,
to the searing flame. His soul departed
2820 the triumph to find of the true and the steadfast.

Then wretched it was for the warrior young,
sad was it for him when he saw on the earth
his lord beloved with his life at an end.
Likewise the slayer lay extended,
2825 the dragon of earth dreadful though lifeless,
overcome with ruin. The coiling serpent
no longer could hold the hoard of treasure,
for it was destroyed by swords of iron,
by battle-notched blades beaten and tempered;
2830 and stilled by its wounds the wide-flying monster
lay stretched on the soil by the side of the cavern.
No more through the sky at midnight, and proud
of the wealth it guarded, its wings it would beat,
revealing its presence, but prone on the earth
2835 it lay by the hand of the hero who slew it.
Few men truly can be found in the world
with strength like his, as searching has taught me,
though bold in adventure and valiant in daring,
who would meet the breath of the monster's venom
2840 or disturb with their hands the hall of its treasure,
for fear lest waking they should find the guard
who dwelt in the barrow. To Beowulf came
abundance of wealth that was won by his death.
Each to the other an end had made
2845 of his fleeting life.

Not long was it then

ere the feeble cowards came from the forest,
the traitorous cravens ten together,
who dared not before fight with their javelins
when great was the need of their gracious lord.
2850 With shame in their mien their shields they bore,
came in their armor where the old man lay.
They looked on Wiglaf. He wearied sat
by the side of his lord, the loyal retainer—
would rouse him with water, but won no response.
2855 The life of his chieftain any longer on earth
he could not stay, though strong his desire,
nor the act of the Lord in any wise change,
for the course of man's life by the counsels of God
was ever controlled, and always must be.
2860 Then the youth gave answer in anger to them
whose courage had failed, to the cowards he scorned;
Wiglaf responded, Weoxstan's son,
the sad-hearted warrior saw and despised them:
'Lo, he who will tell the truth as it is
2865 may say of our lord, who bestowed on you riches
and the trappings of war you are wearing now—
since he on the ale-bench has often given
to his men in the hall helmets and byrnies,
the prince to his thanes whatever most precious
2870 he could find by searching either far or near—
that he has wasted what in war he gained,
all of it grievously, such gear of battle.
The people's king of comrades like you
had no reason to boast. Yet the Ruler of Victory,
2875 the Lord gave him power to punish his foe,
his vengeance to take when valor was needed.
I could do little his life to protect
in the thick of the combat, but I could surpass
the strength that I had to help my kinsman.
2880 The savage enemy was ever the weaker
when I struck with my sword; less strongly belched

from its jaws the fire.   Too few the defenders
who pressed to aid in the prince's need.
The gaining of treasure and the giving of swords,
2385all delight and joy will be lost to your tribe
in their home hereafter, and every man
will forfeit the rights that his father has left him
throughout your whole clan.   Close will this follow
when the nobles have learned the news of your flight,
2890your dastardly deed.   Death is better
for any man left to a life of disgrace.'
      Then he bade carry to the camp on the sea-cliff
word of the battle, to the bearers of shields
who in sadness of heart had sat through the morning,
2895to the warrior band who had waited in hope
of their lord's return, yet in the terror also
lest he meet his death.   He who mounted the head-
      land
did not keep silence, but spoke to all,
uttering truthfully the tale of new sorrow:
2900'The lord of the Geats, the giver of joy
to the Wether folk, has found his last rest;
on the bed of death the dragon has laid him.
Yet the foe who slew him beside him lies
weakened by sword-thrusts, though the sword could
      never
2905by wounds make an end of the enemy monstrous
in any wise.   Wiglaf by Beowulf
is sitting now, the son of Weoxstan,
by his lifeless lord the loyal warrior
is keeping the death-watch with dolorous heart
2910over friend and foe.   Fear to the people
of war shall arise when widely and well
among Franks and Frisians the fall of the king
shall be published abroad.   There broke out hostility
with the Hugs and battle when Hygelac came
2915leading his sea-army to the land of the Frisians,

where the Hetwares met him with a mighty attack,
the victory gained by their greater power
and brought to earth the armored warrior,
who fell in the combat. There came no wealth
2920 from the lord to the army. To us ever after
the Merovingian no mercy has shown.

'From the Swedish people neither peace nor good
    faith
in any way hope I, since Hæthcyn Hrethling,
as widely was known, the noble Ongentheow
2925 bereft of his life at Ravenswood,
when first in their pride a force of the Geats
a battle waged on the warlike Scylfings.
Soon Ohtere's father, wise and aged,
terror-inspiring, turned on his enemy,
2930 cut down the sea-king and saved his wife
the queen, though her jointure and jewels were lost,
the mother of Ohtere and of Onela.
He followed his foes while they fled away
till at length hard-pressed, with their leader gone,
2935 a refuge they found in Ravenswood.
With a mighty force the miserable remnant
sorely wounded he encircled there,
and through the night he threatened the band,
saying often that with the sword at dawn
2940 he would slay them all, though some on the gallows
should be food for the birds. Yet found they help
for their sorrow of heart when they heard in the
    morning
the trumpets and horns of Hygelac sound,
knew that the leader was leaving them not,
2945 but followed after with a force of warriors.
Then the battle was gory between Geats and Swedes,
and wide was the conflict of warriors contending,
when men to the fray with fury were stirred.
The noble Ongentheow anon with his kinsmen,
2950 oppressed by sorrow, sought for a refuge,

withdrew in his prudence to a place far off.
He knew the power of proud Hygelac,
his valor in combat, and he could not trust
his strength to resist the sea-men in battle,
2955 against the raiders his riches to guard,
or the children and women. Went thence retreating
the old king to his fortress, and followed after
the Swedish people the standards of Hygelac,
which overpassed the plain of refuge
2960 till the sons of Hrethel had sought out the fastness.
There was halted the hoary Ongentheow,
was brought to a stand by the swords of his enemy,
and the king of the people came to submission
at Eofor's will. In anger against him
2965 Wulf, son of Wonred, with his weapon struck
till the blood from his veins at the blow sprang out
beneath his gray hair. Yet had no fear
the aged Scylfing, but speedily paid
the folk-king then, when he found his chance,
2970 a mighty return for the murderous stroke.
A blow to counter this could not give back
the brave son of Wonred to the warrior old,
for his helmet was shorn from his head by the sword,
and with blood gushing out he bowed where he stood,
2975 fell prone on the earth. Yet he perished not
but lifted his head though his hurt was sore.
Then the bold thane of Hygelac above the shield-wall
with his broad sword struck where his brother lay,
let his ancient blade, the heirloom of giants,
2980 cleave the great helmet. Thus hurt to his death
the king of the folk fell and perished.
Now the battle was won, to Wulf Wonreding
came many in haste with help to raise him
and to bind his wounds, while his warrior kinsman
2985 Eofor was rifling aged Ongentheow,
from the king was taking his corslet of iron,
his hilted sword and his helmet too,

all his armor, which he offered to Hygelac.
He received those treasures, saying fairly
2990they should find their reward—and fulfilled his
    promise.
The lord of the Geats gave for the exploit,
the son of Hrethel, when home he had come,
to Wulf and to Eofor rewards of great treasure,
to each of them land and linked rings granted
2995worth a hundred thousand, which they held without
    envy,
such fame among men they had found for their
    deeds;
and he gave to Eofor his only daughter
for his honor and pleasure, a pledge of friendship.
'These are the enmities, and this is the feud
3000of warring foes, which fearful make me
lest the Swedish folk will seek us out
when once they have learned that our lord is dead,
he who has guarded against attack
our wealth and our kingdom, has wielded for good
3005the power he held from the heroes who've fallen,
to the bold Sea-Geats has given example
of a warrior's valor. Let us view now in haste
the king of our people, and carry him soon
with fitting rites to the funeral pyre,
3010our giver of rings. Not a remnant only
must burn with the hero, but the hoard of treasure,
the gold uncounted so grievously won,
the rings at the last with his life itself
so dearly bought. By the burning flame
3015they must be enfolded, by the fire devoured.
Never shall warrior wear the jewels
to be a remembrance, nor maiden fair
use their adornment; but destitute, sad,
not a few shall wander in a foreign land
3020now that our leader shall laugh no more
or shout with rejoicing. The spear shall be grasped

in the chill of morning by many hands
and lifted high. No harp with its music
shall rouse the warriors, but the raven dark,
3025 eager for carrion, to the eagle shall cry,
shall tell of the meal he made with the wolf
when they plundered the fallen, supped full on the
    corpses.'
  Thus in bitterness the brave man spoke,
in the words he said concealing naught
3030 nor hiding their fate. The host all arose
and went unhappy with welling tears
to see under Eagleness a sight to marvel at.
The lifeless form they found on the sand,
on his bed of rest their ring-giver lying.
3035 To the warrior-king had come the end,
to the brave the day of death unescapeable,
to the prince of the Wethers a wondrous departure.
Yet first struck their sight a stranger creature,
the dragon stretched on the strand beside him,
3040 a monstrous foe mottled in hue,
a terror to see now scorched by its fire.
As it lay on the earth, the length of its body
was fifty feet. It had flown by night
in the darkness sporting, then down to its den
3045 it had sunk at rest. Now stilled by death
in the caves no more would it make its lair.
By it were standing beakers and goblets,
plates were lying, and precious swords
consumed with rust, which had rested there
3050 for a thousand winters in the womb of earth.
That heritage also of ancient men
was circled about by spells of power,
so that no one ever might enter there
in the hall of gold if from God Himself,
3055 the true King of Victory, the Trust of mankind,
he had not the power the hoard to enter,
and such an one only as seemed to Him meet.

It was known of old that naught was the profit
to him who the treasure hid there wrongfully
3060within the barrow. Ere this the guardian
had slain not a few, the feud pursuing
with savage vengeance. Uncertain it is
when a man of courage shall come to the end
of his destined life and longer may not
3065with his kinsmen inhabit the hall of rejoicing.
So was it with Beowulf when the barrow's guard
he sought in battle: himself he knew not
the way he should part from the world at the last.
Till the day of doom deeply had cursed it
4070the famous princes who had placed the gold there:
that he should suffer for his sin and be fettered
in heathen fanes, in hell be bound,
be punished with torments if he plundered the hoard.
By no means had Beowulf on the booty beforehand
3075looked with envy and the lust for gold.

Now spoke Wiglaf, Weoxstan's son:
'Often a warrior for one who is gone
such woe must suffer as we do now.
We could not persuade our king beloved,
3080the lord of the realm in the least by our counsel
to withhold from the guard of the gold his attack,
to leave him unscathed where long he had rested,
to dwell therein till the end of the world,
fulfilling his destiny. Dire is it for us
3085that the hoard was discovered—too hard is the fate
that impelled the prince to approach the cavern.
I entered there and everything saw,
the wealth of the barrow, since the way was allowed
me
and the duty enjoined, though dreadful the feat.
4090In the hall under earth in haste I seized
what treasure I found, and forth in my hands,
a mighty burden, I bore it hither

to my lord and king. Alive was he still,
aware and conscious. The wise old man
3095 spoke long in his sorrow, said to greet you,
asked that a mighty mound be builded,
lofty and famous as your lord's deeds were,
on the place of his burning a barrow befitting
the warrior on earth most widely honored
3100 while he kept in prosperity his castle and realm.
Now let us hasten anew to seek out
and to view the wealth of wondrous adornments,
the hidden splendor. I will show you the way,
so that right at hand the rings you may see,
3105 the broad plates of gold. Let his bier be made ready
that on coming forth we may find it prepared
and may carry thereon our king and lord,
the man whom we love, and leave him at rest
in the keeping of God Who guides the world.'
3110   Then Weoxstan's son, the warrior bold,
commanded the throng of men with possessions,
the warriors all, that wood for the pyre
they bring from afar to the brave folk-leader,
and lay it beside him: 'Now must fire devour,
3115 as the dark flame waxes, our warror chieftain
who often withstood the shower of iron
when the storm of arrows well aimed from the bow-
            string
passed the wall of shields, and the shaft did its
            service,
the swift barb following the feathers' guidance.'
3120   Then Wiglaf the wise, Weoxstan's son,
of the thanes of the king called on the noblest,
seven together he summoned forth,
and with them he entered the enemy's hall.
One of the warriors, who went before them,
3125 bore a torch in his hand. Heroes were all,
for they chose not by lot who should loot the treasure.
No watchman they saw o'er the wealth of the cavern;

they found it empty in every part,
lying desolate; and little they grieved
3130as they bore out hastily the heaped-up treasure.
The dragon also they dragged to the sea-cliff
and tumbled it over, so that out with the flood
the waves enfolded the warden of jewels.
Then the well-wrought gold on a wagon was laden,
3135the wealth uncounted, and the king was borne,
the aged ruler, to Hronesness.

Then the folk of the Geats a funeral pyre
built on the headland, a bale-fire splendid
hung over with shields, with shining corslets,
3140with helmets of war, as he had desired.
They laid upon it the prince illustrious
with lamentation for their lord so dear;
and the warriors kindled on the cliff-side the flame
of the mighty pyre. Murky the wood-smoke
3145uprose all dark, while roared the fire;
and weeping was heard, but the winds were quiet,
till the heat in its breast the body consumed.
Their hearts were sad, and with sorrow stricken
they lamented the death of their dearly-loved lord.
3150Then an aged woman in her woe for Beowulf,
with her locks bound up, a lay of mourning
sang, and repeated that sorely she feared
days of evil, enmity, slaughter,
the terror of war, and the taking of captives.
3155The heavens consumed the smoke of the pyre.

The folk of the Geats a barrow fashioned,
a mound on the cliff massive and lofty,
to be seen afar by sailors who journeyed,
built it in honor of the brave in battle,
3160in ten days made it in memory of him,
to guard his ashes. Whatever the wise
could find that was noble his name to recall
they bore to the mound: bracelets and jewels,
all the treasure that enemies earlier,

₃₁₆₅men who were hostile, in the hoard had placed;
   resigned the warriors' wealth to the earth,
   the gold to the mound, where yet it remains
   as useless to men as erstwhile it was.
   Then around the barrow there rode together
₃₁₇₀twelve who in battle were bravest and best,
   gave voice to their care, the king lamented,
   chanted their sorrow in a song of grief.
   They praised the might of the man and his deeds,
   sang of the hero as seemly it is
₃₁₇₅that comrades acclaim their king and lord,
   in heart hold him dear when hence from the body
   the hero has left his hearth-companions.
   Thus lamented the men of the Geats
   the death of their lord, for they deemed him to be
₃₁₈₀of the kings of the world the kindest and noblest,
   the gentlest of men, most good to his people,
   acclaimed by all most eager for fame.

CYNEWULF

FROM only two poets of the period before the Norman Conquest have we any verse remaining to which the author's
name can be attached. One of these men is Cædmon,
from whom Bede in his Latin history of the early days
of the British Church quotes a few lines. The other is
Cynewulf, who signed four poems with acrostics, which spell
out his name in runic letters. These are *Juliana, Elene,
Christ,* and *The Fates of the Apostles.* The author cannot
be definitely identified with any Cynewulf of whom we have
knowledge from other sources; but he was certainly an
ecclesiastic who lived in the north of England, and he probably wrote towards the end of the eighth century. Whether
he composed other poems like *The Phoenix, Guthlac,* and

Andreas we do not know. They have similar characteristics. It is more difficult to show in translation the virtues of Cynewulf and his school than of the *Beowulf* poet. Cynewulf was gifted with amazingly keen sense perceptions, and depended largely upon sensory images for his effects. These inevitably become dulled and blurred in a translation. Yet the rhapsodic hymns and emotionalized descriptive scenes of *Christ* have great beauty, while such a poem as *Elene* cannot be ignored by any lover of narrative verse in the heroic manner.

From CHRIST

AN ADVENT HYMN

O radiant and glorious, Thou God exalted,
Thou High and Holy, heavenly Trinity!
Broad creation brings its praises;
and rightfully should we, though wretched mortals,
our voices lift to laud and honor,
to give Thee praise, since God the faithful
has shown Himself, the Savior, to us.
Aloft in heaven the holy Seraphim,
the true and brave, in throngs unwearying,
10 among the angels ever with their praises
raise songs to Thee and sound aloud,
both near and far, fairly with their voices
their hymns cf joy. They have of duties
the noblest to the King, for Christ has granted
that they may ever with their eyes behold Him,
may there adore, celestially adorned,
the Lord Who rules through regions without end.
And with their wings they guard our God eternal,
the majesty and glory of the mighty Lord;
20 and ever round His throne they throng, for each
    desires
with fluttering wing to fly the nearest
our King and Savior in the courts of peace.

The Well-beloved they laud, and in the light He
          spreads
they sing these words and sound His praises,
Creator glorious of all created things:
'Holy art Thou, holy, of the hosts of the arch-
          angels
very Lord and Prince! The Victor art Thou, holy,
Lord of Lords forever! Everlasting shall endure
Thy glory in the world, and widely honored
till time is gone, for Thou art God of hosts,
and earth and heaven are ever filled,
10 O Guard of warriors, with the glory of Thy pres-
          ence,
O Protector all-powerful! Eternal be
in the highest heights Thy glory, and in earth Thy
          praise
be bright forever! O blest and loved
Who comes to men, to give comfort to the wretched
in the name of Him Who in the heights shall have
praises without ending, everlasting honor!'

From ELENE

CONSTANTINE'S VISION AND BATTLE
WITH THE HUNS

Of the circling years, counted by number,
two hundred and thirty and three had passed,
and so many winters that measure the world,
20 since God the Ruler, the Glory of kings,
the Light of the faithful, in the form of man
was born on earth. The sixth it was
of Constantine's rule in the realm imperial,
since as leader of war in the land of the Romans
he was raised to command. To his men he was
          gracious,

his people's protector, and of praise he was eager.
The realm of the prince, which he ruled under
 heaven,
grew mighty withal. He made it great,
for a true king was he, and a help in battle
to the warriors all. For his worth God blessed him
with glory and power; and he gave to many
his comfort and aid through the earth far and wide;
did vengeance on foes when violence stirred him
to lift his weapons.
10   Then war was proclaimed,
the terror of battle. There were thronging hosts,
the folk of the Huns, and the Hrethgoth people,
while forth there came the Franks and the Hugs.
Brave were the warriors and bold for fighting;
their lances gleamed, and their linked mail glittered.
With shouts and the clash of clattering shields
the heroes raised on high their standard,
assembled in force; and forth together
came marching the host. In the midst of the forest
20 the wolf gave voice and of violence chanted,
while the dewy-winged eagle on the enemies' track
sang of slaughter to be. The soldiers to battle
moved fast, to attack the fortified places,
as mighty a concourse as the King of the Huns
could in any way summon from all his neighbors
of warriors to battle. So went they forth,
the finest of armies, with foot and with horse;
marched to the Danube, and made their camp
in that alien land, those lancers brave,
30 by the surge of the water with sound and with
 tumult.
They would ruin the realm of the Romans, and
 sack it
with their plundering hosts.

Then the Huns' approach
became known in the city. Caesar commanded
to summon the soldiers in squadron formation
against the foe, and to form at once
the army for battle, to bring forth for conflict
the warriors in haste under heaven's arch.
Valiant and eager for victory were they,
the dwellers in Rome, and ready they made them
with their weapons for war, though weaker their
    forces
10 in number and power for the press of the combat
than those that came riding with the King of the
    Huns.
But their bucklers clashed, and clattered their shields.
The King with his troop, with his conquering host,
led them to battle. Aloft the dark raven,
greedy for carrion, cried from the heavens.
To the marching host the heralds gave orders,
the trumpeters ran, and the tread of the horses
on the earth was loud. Eager for battle
the army came; but the King was afraid,
20 troubled with care, when the throng he saw
of Huns and of Hreths, as his host he collected
at the river's bank on the bounds of his kingdom.
The King of the Romans was racked with care,
lest for lack of men he should lose his realm.
Too few were his warriors, too frail his support
against the might overpowering he must meet in
    battle.
    Near the river waited the warriors and leader
for the space of a night, after sighting first
the host assembled. Then to Caesar a dream
30 was revealed in his slumber, as he slept with his
    men;
longing for victory, a vision he saw.
A beauteous being, brilliant and shining,

in form like a man, but far more splendid
than ever before under the arch of heaven
he had seen with his eyes, it seemed there appeared.
His head he raised, the helmeted warrior,
and the angel spoke, the envoy of glory,
the messenger radiant, called the man by name
in haste, while the darkness grew dim and was light.
    'The King of the angels, Constantine, greets you,
the Lord of Hosts, Who allots our destinies.
10 He offers a covenant, so fear not at all,
though the foreign host make a fearful threat
of battle hard.   To the heavens look
on the Warden of glory; there weal you shall find,
a sign of victory.'   Then soon he obeyed
the behest of the holy one; his heart he opened,
and he gazed on high, as had given command
the beauteous angel.   There brightly adorned
the Tree of Glory, with rich gold gleaming,
he saw in the heavens, splendid with jewels.
20 And words were written on the radiant Cross,
shining and brilliant: 'In this sign you will conquer
the host of your foes in the fearful battle,
will hinder and let them.'   Then the light departed
and vanished away, and with it the angel
to the host of the blessed.   But blither the ruler,
the more free of care the King in his heart
because of the sight he had seen so fair.
    Then the lord of nobles a likeness commanded
of that he had seen there in the heavens;
30 the famous king, Constantine bade them
to make in haste, the mighty ruler,
the giver of rings, a Rood of Christ
as a symbol and token of the sight in the vision.
In the twilight gray he gave his commands
to awaken the warriors for the battle of weapons,
to raise the standards, and the Rood all holy

to bear before them as the beacon of God,
to carry it forward when the foe they attacked.
 Loud the trumpets sang as they surged on the
  enemy;
the raven grew eager, and the eagle damp-winged
gazed at the conflict of cruel warriors;
the wolf gave tongue, the woodland companion.
The battle arose. There was rushing of warriors
and clashing of shields, combat furious
and the slaying of men when they met the arrow-
  flight.
10 In showers the arrows, over shields the spears
they sent on the doomed and desperate foe;
on the enemy bold the battle-adders
they speeded forth by the strength of their hands.
They advanced strong-hearted, they hastened forward,
tore shields asunder and their spears thrust in,
pressed forward boldly. Then the banner was
  raised,
the standard before them, and they sang of victory.
The golden helmets gleamed like the lances
on the field of, battle. Fell there the barbarous;
20 the heathen perished. The Hun folk at once
fled on beholding the Holy Tree
which the King of the Romans had reared in battle.
Widely were scattered the warriors bold.
Some in the conflict were killed with weapons;
some saved their lives, but saved them hardly,
by their sudden flight; and some half dead
fled to a fastness, and found there refuge
in the rocky cliffs, reaching the Danube
and a strong place near it; while some in the stream
30 were drowned as they swam, and their doom there
  met.
 Then the host of the brave was happy and joyous;

pursued the aliens until evening came
at the end of day, while the darts still flew,
the adders of battle. The enemy perished,
the force of the foe, for few went thence
of the host of the Huns to their homes again.
Then was it clear that Constantine
the King Almighty had made the victor,
had endowed him with honor in the day of battle,
with rule under heaven through His Rood Tree there,

THE WANDERER *

APART from heroic poems of various sources, and such inno-
vations as we associate with Cynewulf, the best things surviving from the wreckage of Old English literature are a
few poems in the elegiac mood. Of these *The Wanderer*
is the most striking and poignant. It was probably written
in the eighth century. Like almost all the Old English verse
that is left, it has come down to us in a single manuscript,
which has been preserved in Exeter Cathedral since about
the time of the Norman Conquest.

10 Many a lonely man at last comes to honor,
   Merits God's mercy, though much he endured
   On wintry seas, with woe in his heart,
   Dragging his oar through drenching-cold brine,
   Homeless and houseless and hunted by Wyrd.

   These are the words of a way-faring wanderer,
   This is his song of the sorrow of life,
   Slaughter of foemen, felling of kinsmen:

   * From Old English Poetry by J. Duncan Spaeth. By permission
of Princeton University Press, publishers.

Oft in the dark alone, before dawning,
All to myself my sorrow I tell.
No friend have I here to whom I may open
My heart's deep secret, my hidden spring of woe.
Well do I know 'tis the way of the high-born,
Fast in his heart to fetter his feelings,
Lock his unhappiness in the hold of his mind.
Spirit that sorrows withstandeth not destiny,
Heart that complaineth plucketh no help.
10 A haughty hero will hide his suffering,
Manfully master misery's pang.
Thus stricken with sorrow, stript of my heritage,
Far from kinsmen and country and friends,
Grimly I grappled my grief to my bosom,
Since long time ago, my giver of bounty
Was laid in the earth, and left me to roam
Watery wastes, with winter in my heart.
Forsaken I sought a shielder and protector;
Far and near I found none to greet the wanderer,
20 No master to make him welcome in his wine-hall:
None to cheer the cheerless, or the friendless to
      befriend.

He who has lost all his loved companions
Knoweth how bitter a bedfellow is sorrow.
Loneliness his lot, not lordly gold,
Heart-chilling frost, not harvest of plenty.
Oft he remembers the mirth of the mead-hall,
Yearns for the days of his youth, when his dear
      lord
Filled him with abundance. Faded are those joys!
He shall know them no more; no more shall he
      listen
30 To the voice of his lord, his leader and counsellor.
Sometimes sleep and sorrow together
Gently enfold the joyless wanderer:

Bright are his dreams, he embraces his lord again,
Kisses his liege, and lays on his knee
Head and hands as in happy days,
When he thanked for a boon his bountiful giver.
Wakes with a start the wanderer homeless;
Nought he beholds but the heaving surges,
Seagulls dipping and spreading their wings,
Scurries of snow and the scudding hail.
Then his heart is all the heavier,
10 Sore after sweet dreams sorrow reviveth.
Fain would he hold the forms of his kinsmen,
Longingly leans to them, lovingly greets them;
Slowly their faces swim into distance;
No familiar greeting comes from the fleeting
Companies of kinsmen. Care ever shadows
The way of the traveller, whose track is on the
        waters,
Whose path is on the billows of the boundless deep.

Behold I know not how I may keep
My heart from sinking, heavy with sorrow,
20 When all life's destiny deeply I ponder,—
Men that are suddenly snatched in their prime,
High-souled heroes; so the whole of this earth
Day by day droopeth and sinketh to decay. . .
How dread is the doom of the last desolation,
When all the wealth of the world shall be waste,
He that is wise may learn, if he looks
Abroad o'er this land, where lonely and ruinous,
Wind-swept walls, waste are standing;
Tottering towers, crusted with frost,
30 Crumbling wine-halls, bare to the sky.
Dead is their revelry, dust are the revellers!
Some they have fallen on far fields of battle,
Some have gone down in ships on the sea;
Some were the prey of the prowling gray-wolf,

Some by their loved ones were laid in the earth.
The Lord of the living hath levelled their mansions,
Silenced the sound of the singing and laughter.
Empty and bare are all their habitations,
Wondrous works of the giants of old.

He that considers this scene of desolation,
And this dark life deeply doth ponder,—
Battle and blood-shed, burning and slaughter,
10 It bringeth to mind, and mournfully he asks:
Where is the warrior, where is the war-horse?
Where is the giver of bounty, where are the boon·
    companions,
The "dream and the gleam" that gladdened the hall?
Alas the bright ale-cup, alas the brave warrior!
Alas the pride of princes! Their prime is no more;
Sunk under night's shadow, as though it had never
    been!
Where lusty warriors thronged, this lone wall
    towers,
Weird with dragon-shapes, wondrously carven;
Storm of ash-spears hath stricken the heroes,
20 Blood-thirsty weapons, Wyrd the supreme.
Wintry blasts now buffet these battlements;
Dreary snow-storms drift up the earth,
The terror of winter when wild and wan
Down from the north with the darkness drives
The ruinous scourge of the ruthless hail.

All this life is labor and sorrow,
Doom of destiny darkens o'er earth.
Wealth is fleeting, friends are fleeting,
Man is fleeting, maid is fleeting,
30 All this earth's foundations utterly shall pass.

THE VISION OF PIERS PLOWMAN

OF THE poets who had a part in the remarkable revival of writing in English, which came about during the second half of the fourteenth century, one of the most interesting is the unknown author of *The Vision of Piers Plowman.* This work used to be confidently ascribed to a William Lang-land, about whom a biography was built up which is now seen to have been based on quite insufficient evidence. Three different versions of the poem exist. Version A consists of a prologue and twelve sections, or passus, and contains 2567 lines. The following translation is from this text. Version B is much longer, 4242 lines in all, and includes nine sections not in the A-text. Version C is a still more expanded form, consisting of 7357 lines. It is the present belief of scholars that the poem was first written in 1362 or soon afterward, that the B-text was composed in 1376 or 1377, and that the final version appeared in the last decade of the century. Opinions differ as to whether or not the man who first made the poem was also responsible for the longer forms of it.

Such unsettled problems need not blind us, however, to the importance of the work. Unquestionably the first author was one of greatest satirists who have ever written in English, and he produced one of the best allegorical visions of all time. He must have known London well; but he chose as his medium the old alliterative verse that had sprung into vogue in the west and north of England with the contemporary growth of national consciousness, and he used language that smacked of the country—used it, prob-ably, with the conscious intention of making his poem seem rustic. Unlike Chaucer, whom he resembles in his powers of observation, the author was aflame with moral indignation against the evils of his time. He was too gener-ous and too large-hearted to be a crabbed commentator, but he lacked no vigor in his denunciation of wickedness and folly. As a vision, his poem has the merit of moving the characters across the scene in a wholly dreamlike fashion; as an allegory, it rivals the work of Bunyan in clearness of visualization and sharpness of outline; as a satire, it compares favorably in vividness of detail and picturesqueness of phrase with anything in the language. No writer has ever expounded more ably the virtues of honesty and common sense and simple faith.

In a summer season when soft was the sun,
I got me the garments and garb of a shepherd,
Like those of a hermit unholy of works,
And wandered wide through the world wonders to
    hear.
But on a May morning on the Malvern Hills
A marvel befell me, a fairy thing, it seemed.
I was weary from wandering and went to take rest
By the side of a brook where the bank was wide;
And there as I lay and looked at the waters,
10 I dropped off to sleep, the sound was so pleasant.
    Then began I to dream a dream that was mar-
      vellous,
That I was in a wilderness, but where I could not
    tell.
As I looked to the east where aloft rose the sun,
I saw a splendid tower set on a hill,
With a deep dale below it, and a dungeon therein,
With a deep and dark ditch dreadful to see.
    A fair field full of folk found I between them,
Of all manner of men, both the mean and the rich,
Working and wandering as the world compels.
20 Some were at the plough and played full seldom,
Labored full hard as they harrowed and sowed,
Worked for what these wasters in gluttony destroy.
    And some were very proud and apparelled ac-
      cordingly,
Cleverly disguised by the cut of their clothing,
While many were praying and doing their penance,
For the love of Our Lord living full hard,
Like anchorites and hermits who hold them in their
    cells
And care not to wander the country about

To get a fat livelihood and feed up their bodies.
  And some bought and sold, the better to thrive,
As it seems to our thinking that such men should.
And some made mirth as minstrels know how,
And got gold by their glee—guiltlessly, I trow.
But jesters and clowns, the children of Judas,
Mimicked and mimed, and made themselves fools,
Though they had wit enough to work if they wished.
Paul preaches of them, though I stay not to prove it:
10 *Qui loquitur turpiloquium* he is Lucifer's servant.
  Mendicants and beggars went about their business
  Till their bags and their bellies were brimful
      crammed;
Whined for their food and fought at the ale-house,
Going to bed in gluttony, God knows the truth is,
And rising up with ribaldry, these knaves of Robert.
Sleepiness and sloth pursue them forever.
  Pilgrims and palmers plighted together
To seek St. James of Spain and the saints in Rome;
Went upon their way with many a wise tale,
20 And had leave to lie all their lives thereafter.
Hermits, a heap of them, with hooks on their staves,
Were walking to Walsingham—each had his wench
      with him.
Husky tall lubbers who were loath to labor
Clothed themselves in copes, and called themselves
      brothers;
And some became hermits simply for idleness.
  I found there the friars, all the four orders,
Preaching to the people for the profit of their bellies,
Twisting the Gospel as it seemed good to them,
Construing it badly to bring a new cope,
30 For many of these masters may dress as it pleases
      them,
Since money and their merchandise meet together
      often.

Now that charity has turned chapman, and chiefly
    shrives lords,
Many wonders have befallen within a few years.
Unless Holy Church begin to hold herself better,
The greatest mischief on earth will mount up fast.
   There preached a pardoner as though he were a
    priest,
And pulled out a bull with a bishop's seals on it,
Said that he himself could assoil them all
From falsehood and fasting, and from the vows
    they had broken.
The ignorant liked him and believed what he said,
10 Came up and kneeled and kissed his bull.
   He banged them with his bull and bleared their
    eyes,
So his bull brought to him brooches and rings.
Thus you give your gold for gluttony's sustenance,
Turn it over to fellows who follow after lechery.
Were the bishop truly blessed and worthy of both
    his ears,
They would not be so bold in bamboozling the
    people.
Yet do not blame the bishop that the beggar preaches,
For the parish priest and he go halves on the silver
That poor folk would have if it were not for them.
20   Parsons and parish priests complain to their
    bishops
That their parishes are poor since the time of the
    pestilence,
And ask leave and licence to live up in London
And sing masses for simony, since silver is sweet.
   Then appeared a hundred in hoods of silk;
Sergeants they seemed, who serve at the bar
And plead the law for pence, or pounds more likely,
But never for the love of God will unloose their
    lips.

You might better meet the mist on the Malvern
    Hills
Than get a mumble from their mouths till money is
    shown.
I saw there bishops bold and bachelors of divinity,
Who had turned accounting clerks in the king's
    service.
There were deacons and archdeacons, whose duty it
    was
To preach to the people and the poor to feed,
Who went loping off to London by leave of their
    bishops
To be clerks of the King's Bench for the country's
    harm.
    Barons and burgesses and bondmen, too,
10 I saw in that assembly, as you shall hear hereafter.
There were bakers and butchers and brewsters
    aplenty,
Female woolen weavers and weavers of linen,
Tailors and fullers and tanners among them,
Masons and miners and men of other crafts,
Ditchers and delvers who do their work ill
And pass the long day with "Dieu vous save, Dame
    Emma!"
    Cooks and their knaves cry "Hot pies! Hot!
Good geese and pigs! Go dine! Go!"
Tavern-keepers with them told the same tale
20 About good wine of Gascony and wine of Alsace,
Of Rochelle and the Rhine, the roast to digest.
All this I saw while sleeping, and seven times more.

Passus I

What the mountain means and the dark dale be-
    neath it,
And the fair field full of folk, fairly I will show you.

A very lovely lady garbed all in linen
Came down from the cliff and called to me cour-
teously,
Saying "Son, do you sleep? Do you see these
people,
How busy they are about the foolish maze?
The great part of the people who pass their lives
on earth
Have their reward in this world and wish for noth-
ing better;
Of any other heaven they have no care at all."
   I was afraid when I saw her, though fair was ner
face,
And said "I thank you, madam. What does all this
mean?"
10 "This hill and this tower," quoth she, "truth dwells
therein;
And would that you wrought as His word teaches.
For he is Father of our faith, who formed you
wholly
Both with skin and with features, and gave you five
wits
To worship Him therewith the while you dwell here.
He made the earth for you to match all your needs
With woolen and linen, and a living to give you;
Within measure, moreover, to make you at ease.
He decreed in his courtesy three things in common,
And what their names are it is needful that I tell
you,
20 Rehearsing them in order by rule and by reason.
The one thing is clothing to keep you from the cold,
The second meat at meals to keep you from misery,
And the third drink when thirsty, but drink not
out of reason.
   "For Lot in his lifetime, because of liking for
drink,

Did with his daughters what the devil loved;
Took delight in drink as the devil wished,
And so fell into lechery and lay with them both.
He said that the wine he drank made him do the
wicked deed.
Take care of pleasant drink, and you will come off
better;
Be moderate in all things, no matter how you yearn.
What the body longs for is not always best for
spirit,
Nor pleasing to the body what is pleasant to the soul.
Do not believe your body, for a liar misleads it,
10 Which is the wicked world that works to betray you.
The fiend and your flesh follow on together,
And your soul will destroy unless you search your
heart.
For your better guidance I give you this counsel."
    "I thank you, madam," quoth I. "Your words
    please me well.
But what of the money that men hold so fast?
Tell me to whom the treasure belongs."
"Go to the Gospel," quoth she. "What did God
Himself say
When the people in the temple placed a penny before
Him,
And asked if they should honor Caesar as their
king?
20 He asked them in turn the teaching of the letters,
And whose was the image that was printed thereon.
'It is Caesar,' they said, 'as all of us can see.'
'Then *Reddite*,' quoth God, 'what to Caesar belongs,
Et que sunt dei deo, or else you do a wrong.'
For rightful reasoning should rule you in all things,
And native wit be warden and keeper of your
wealth,

The guardian of it, to give it you at need.
Thrift and common sense thrive well together."

Then I questioned humbly by Him Who made
her:

"The dungeon in the dale that dreadful is to see,
What does that mean, madam? I beg you to tell
me."

"That is Care's castle," quoth she, "and he who
goes therein
May curse that he was born in body or in soul.
Therein dwells a wight who is called Wrong,
The father of falsehood. He founded it himself.

10 Adam and Eve he urged to do wickedness;
Gave counsel to Cain to kill his brother;
Judas he deceived with the Jews' silver
And on an elder tree hanged him thereafter.
He keeps men from love, and lies to all of them
Who trust in their treasure, where is no truth at all."

Then I wondered in mind what woman it was
Who such wise words of Holy Writ showed me.
I begged her by the name of God before she went
away
To give me her name, since she guided me so well.

20 "Holy Church am I," she quoth. "You ought
to know me.
I received you at first and the faith taught you.
You brought me sponsors who promised your obedi-
ence,
That you would love me loyally while your life
endured."

Then I knelt on my knees and cried for her grace,
Praying her piteously to pray for our sins
And also to teach me to trust in Christ,
That I might work His will Who wrought me a
man.

"Give me no treasure, but tell me this only,
How I may save my soul, since a saint you are held.'
    "When all treasures are tested, truth is the best.
I base it on *Deus Caritas,* deeming it right.
It is something as precious as dear God Himself.
Whoso is true with his tongue and tells nothing but
        truth,
Does his work thereby, and does no man ill,
He is reckoned on earth and in heaven to be
        righteous,
And like to our Lord, by St. Luke's words.
10 Clerks who know truth should teach it widely,
For Christians and pagans both lay claim to it.
    "All kings and knights should carefully rule,
And by right should journey about through the
        realm,
Taking trespassers and tying them fast
Until Truth has probed the trespass to the bottom.
For David in his days dubbed him knights,
Made them swear on their swords to serve Truth
        always.
That is the true profession that pertains to knights,
And not to fast one Friday in five score years,
But to hold with him and with her who desire the
        truth,
And for love or for gift never to leave it.
He who fails in that point is apostate to his order.
Christ, the King of Kings, gave knighthood to ten,
Cherubim and Seraphim in all the four orders,
And gave them mastery and might in His majesty,
Making them archangels over all His host,
And taught them through the Trinity the truth to
        know,
To be obedient to His word, but bade them nothing
        else.

"Lucifer learned truth with his legions in heaven,
Being loveliest to see after our Lord,
Until he disobeyed through boasting and pride.
Then fell he with his fellows, and they fiends became;
Thrust from heaven into hell, they were hobbled fast,
Some in air and some in earth and some in depths of hell.
But Lucifer the lowest lies of them all;
For the pride that he showed, his pain has no end.
And all who work evil they shall wend, be sure,
10 After their death day and dwell with the rascal.
But those who keep the word that Holy Writ teaches
And end their lives, as I have said, in meritorious works,
May be sure that their souls shall be saved in heaven,
Where Truth is with the Trinity and shall set them all on thrones.
For I say certainly by the sight of the texts,
When all treasure is tested, truth is the best.
Let ignorant men learn it, since the lettered know it now,
That truth is the treasure most trustworthy on earth."
"I have no native knowledge," quoth I. "You must teach me better,
20 By what power it begins, and where in my body."
"You are doting and a fool," quoth she; "dull are your wits.
It is native knowledge that makes known to your heart
To love your lord liefer than yourself,

And no deadly sin to do, though you die for it.
This, I trow, is truth! Whoso can teach you better
Let him tell you about it and afterward teach others!
Thus His word teaches—and according to it live—
That love is the dearest thing that our Lord asks,
And the plant of peace, too. Preach it with your
harp
When you are merry at your feasts and when men
bid you sing.
For by natural knowledge you may know what to
sing.
That comes from the Father Who formed us all.
10 He looked on us with love and let His Son die
Meekly for our sins, and to amend us all.
Yet He wished them no woe who brought the pain
for Him,
But meekly with His mouth He besought mercy for
them,
Pity for the people who tortured Him to death.
"Here may you see an example in Himself.
Though strong, He was meek, and mercy showed to
them
Who hanged Him high and His heart pierced
through.
And so I charge the rich to have ruth on the poor.
Though mighty you be, be meek in your works.
20 *Eadem mensura qua mensi fueritis, remecietur vobis.*
For the same measure you mete, amiss or otherwise,
You shall be weighed therewith when you wend
hence.
Though you be true of tongue and true in your
winnings,
And as chaste as a child that wails in church,
Unless you live truly and also love the poor,
And give of such goods as God may you send,
You have no more merit in masses and in hours

Than Malkin in her maidenhead which no man de-
    sires.
For the gentle James put it in his book
That faith without works is feebler than naught,
And dead as a door-nail unless the deed follow.
Chastity without charity, know you right well,
Is as useless as a lamp that has no light in it.
Many chaplains are chaste, but charity fails them;
No men are harder when higher they rise,
Unkind to their kin and to all Christian men.
10 They chew up their charity and chide the more
    afterward.
Such chastity without charity may be claimed by
    hell!
    "Curates who keep themselves clean in their bodies
Are so cumbered with cares that they cannot creep
    out,
For avarice holds them bound hard and fast.
That is no truth of the Trinity but the treachery of
    hell,
An example to the ignorant to be niggardly, too.
These are the words that are written in the gospel,
Date et dabitur vobis, for I deal out to all
Your favor and your fortune in finding a livelihood;
20 Wherefore make your acknowledgment out of what
    I have sent.
The key of love is this, to release my grace
For the comfort of the troubled who are cumbered
    with sin.
Love is the chief thing that our Lord asks
And the straight way, too, that leads into heaven.
So I say as before, having seen these texts,
When all treasures are tested, truth is the best.
Now that I have told what truth is, that no treasure
    is better,
I may no longer stay.   May the Lord keep you!"

THE AUTHOR OF *THE PEARL* AND *SIR GAWAIN*

APART from Chaucer, the most accomplished English poet of the fourteenth century was his contemporary, the unknown author of *The Pearl*, who with good reason is thought to have written also *Sir Gawain and the Green Knight*, together with two or three less important works. Who he was has not been discovered, but he must have been writing in the last quarter of the century. Like Chaucer, he knew both books and the ways of the world. There is evidence of his acquaintance not only with Latin literature and the French poetry which was still the birthright of Englishmen, but with the new Italian masters, Dante and Boccaccio; and he was equally familiar with the aristocratic manners, conversation, and sports of his time. The ideals of chivalry and its fine-spun courtesies are mirrored in his verse, as well as the eager aspirations of men who sought at once earthly honor and heavenly comfort. Curiously enough, since he was so learned a person and so accomplished an artist, he chose to write in the dialect of remote Lancashire at just the time when the speech of London was coming to be generally current.

In metrical form *The Pearl* is the most elaborate elegy in English, as can be seen from the following translation of the opening stanzas; but it is no mere exercise in versification. Only a poet with the power of expressing profound feeling in images of beauty could have made it what it is. The appeal to all the senses is sharp, but the appeal is used to stimulate more complicated emotions. Seldom has the beauty of poetic language been so well combined with beauty of formal design. *Sir Gawain and the Green Knight* is equally admirable in another way, being our best English example of the pure mediæval romance. The reader who comes to it for the first time will be struck by the strangeness of the tale: the interweaving of fantastic adventure with sophisticated courtly manners. He will find, if he looks more carefully, that the story is told with exquisite art. Each incident is given its due emphasis, and suspense is maintained to the end with the greatest skill. The loyalty test, which is the main plot, leads so naturally to the secondary plot that the transition is scarcely noticed. Even the elaborate hunting scenes of the third part are justified by the purpose they serve by way of foils to the experiences of Gawain with Bercilak's lady. Another point to observe is that the characters, though thinly drawn as is proper in a romance, always behave like real human beings throughout their amazing adventures. The poet, furthermore, understood the art of using atmosphere to heighten the effect of his story. Not until the age of Burns and Wordsworth can another verse narrative be found in which there is so careful an adaptation of setting to the moods of the characters involved. That such a poem suffers by prose translation must not be forgotten, but certain of its values cannot well be destroyed by the unfortunate necessities of such a rendering.

From THE PEARL

Pearl, formed to be a prince's pride
When chastely set in purest gold,
Came never from the Orient wide
One worthy to be so extolled,
So round, so radiant—every side—
So delicate and smooth to hold!
When gems a judgment must abide,
To set mine first I dared be bold.
Alas! upon a green it rolled
10 Through grass to ground; I marked it not.
And now my grief cannot be told
For my pearl without a stain or spot.

Since in that spot it sprang from me,
Oft have I waited, wished to feel
The joy that erst could set me free
Of baleful chance and bring me weal;
Yet still that comfort cannot be,
Nor solace come my wounds to heal.
But once in thought I seemed to see
20 A vision that began to steal
Upon my heart like music's peal.

Though sad that clay my gem should blot.
O earth, thy stain hath set a seal
On my dear pearl without one spot!

That spot of spices needs must spread
Where wealth like that to earth is run;
Blossoms pale and blue and red
Shine there full bright beneath the sun;
Flower and fruit may there be fed
By the jewel wrapped in earth-folds dun.
10 For each herb grows from seed struck dead;
No wheat were else for harvest won.
From good all good is aye begun;
So that fair seed can fail us not.
Of spices rich shall want not one
From that precious pearl without a spot.

To that spot, then, as it befell,
I entered, to that sheltered green,
In August on a festival,
When corn is cut with sickles keen.
20 The hillock where my pearl once fell
Was pied with flowers sheer and sheen:
Gilliflower, ginger, and gromwell,
And peonies scattered all between.
Fair sight it was that there was seen
And sweet the perfume there, I wot,
Where rests in honor, as I ween,
My precious pearl without a spot.

Before that spot I wrung my hands;
Upon me swept care's swift increase;
30 My heart redoubled its demands
Though reason counselled me to peace.
I wailed my pearl's imprisoning bands,
Complained, and prayed for her release.

Although I knew Christ's mercy stands,
My wretched will I sought to please.
But there I found a strange surcease,
Such fragrance to my brain there shot;
I swooned upon the turf—and these
My visions—pearl without one spot!

From that spot my spirit sprang in space,
My body rested there behind;
My ghost went forth by God's good grace
10 To seek adventures He designed.
I knew not where in earth it was,
But all the place with cliffs was lined;
Towards a wood I turned my face
Where splendid rocks were clear defined.
The light of them could be divined
By no man—a gleaming glory they.
For ne'er were fabrics, to my mind,
Of half their radiance in array.

Arrayed were all the hill-slopes high
20 With cliffs of crystal clear of hue;
A forest bright about them nigh,
With tree boles of the Indies' blue.
Like burnished silver, flung awry,
Leaves quivered in the breeze that blew,
When shafts of sunlight swift to fly
Their shimmering darts intensely threw.
The gravel thick they seemed to strew
With orient pearls like dawn of day;
The very sunbeams paler grew
30 Before their radiance of array.

The sweet array of the hill-sides there
Made my heart's sorrow swift retreat;
The fresh and fruity perfumes were

Refreshment to me like strong meat.
Birds fluttered through the woodland air,
Flame-hued the dusky shadows beat.
The citole and the cithern ne'er
Their mirth could mock, and ne'er defeat;
For when they sang, those birds could cheat
The heart from grief to dance and play,
So gracious were they and so feat
To hear and see in their array.

10 Thus sweetly was arrayed the wood
Where fortune chanced that I should go.
The glory of it no man could
With tongue declare, and none can know
How joyously I strayed, or stood
Even the threatening cliffs below.
The farther, the fairer! Ah, how good
To see the flowers, row on row!
Green hedges and rich rivers show
With golden banks where I might stray.
20 To a stream I won and watched its flow.
Lord, glorious was its array!

The dear array of that great deep
Was a bank as green as beryl bright;
I saw the rushing waters sweep
With murmuring music, running aright.
In the river's bed, where the shadows sleep,
Gleamed stones like the glow through glass of
        light;
Like the streaming stars, when all men sleep,
That glitter aloft in the wintry night.
30 Each pebble that in the pool was pight
Emerald or sapphire I saw display;
The whole deep glowed to my wondering sight,
So precious and proud was its array.

That glory rare of down and dale,
Of wood and water and proud plain,
Brought me to bliss and eased my bale,
O'ercame my grief, destroyed my pain.
Joyous I sped adown the vale
Of that bright stream with surging brain;
And still the greater, without fail,
My joyance grew and did not wane.
For fortune fares as she is fain
10 To grant of weal or woe a store;
And when she favors, one may gain
Delight unceasing, more and more.

More joy came to me in that wise
Than I could tell, though space I had,
For mortal heart may not suffice
To the tenth part of that gladness glad.
Methought in truth that Paradise
Was on those slopes so richly clad;
Methought the river a device
20 To mark the pleasances there made
Beyond it; yet my heart grew sad
To find no crossing there before,
For the water was deep—I durst not wade.
I longed to pass, aye more and more.

Yet more and more I longed to dare
The stream, the while those slopes I scanned;
For though the vale I trod was fair,
Yet lovelier far was yonder land.
Round I began to search and stare
30 To find some ford where I might stand,
Yet of more dangers was I ware,
The farther I strode along the strand.
Was I then from that glory banned
That waited me on the farther shore?

Then came a wondrous thing to hand
That moved my mind aye more and more.

A greater marvel came to light!
I saw beyond that river clear
A cliff of crystal shining bright,
And at its foot I saw appear
A child who gleamed in purest white;
A maiden was she debonair,
And all in glistening raiment dight.
10 I knew her well—I had no fear—
She seemed of glittering gold; all sheer
And shining on the farther shore.
The longer I looked upon her there,
I knew her the better, more and more.

The more I gazed on her fair face,
Her lovely form, a glory came;
Transporting joy began to race
Throughout my heart; and her to name
I longed. Yet for a moment's space
20 The syllables I could not frame
To call her: in so strange a place
She came to me, yet seemed the same.
Her brow that ivory put to shame
She lifted towards me as of yore.
My heart, amazed, could but exclaim—
And ever, as I looked, the more.

SIR GAWAIN AND THE GREEN KNIGHT

When the siege and assault of Troy had come
to an end, and the city destroyed and burnt to
brands and ashes, the man responsible for the
treason there was tried for his treachery, the com-
pletest on earth. It was the noble Æneas with his

5-6

mighty kindred, who afterwards conquered provinces in the Western Isles and became lords of almost all the wealth therein. When noble Romulus came to Rome forthwith, he built that city with great pride, first of all, and named it from his own name, as it is now called; Ticius came to Tuscany and began settlements; Langobard in Lombardy set up homes; and far across the French Sea Felix Brutus joyfully established Britain on many a wide shore,
10 where war and trouble and marvel have appeared by turns, and both happiness and turmoil have often interchanged very quickly ever since.

When Britain had been established by this noble ruler, valiant men were bred there, who loved strife and in the course of time frequently stirred up trouble. More marvels have befallen here in this land than in any other that I know, ever since that day. But of all the kings of Britain who have dwelt here, Arthur was in all ways the noblest, as I
20 have heard. Therefore I intend to recount an adventure that some men hold to be a marvel: something exceeding strange among the wonderful tales about Arthur. If you will listen to this lay for a little while, I will tell it straightforwardly, as I have heard it narrated and as it is set forth and written, brave and strong, wrought into a narrative that has long been known in the land. — 36

The king lay at Camelot during Christmas with many gracious lords, his best knights, all the noble
30 brethren of the Round Table, namely, enjoying splendid revel and unhampered mirth. There at times full many heroes journeyed, and gentle knights jousted full gallantly, then went to the court to dance and sing carols. For there the feast continued without interruption for full fifteen days, with all the banqueting and mirth that men could

devise, merry-making loud and glorious to hear, a pleasant din by day and dancing by night. All was at the peak of happiness for the lords and ladies, whatever they most enjoyed. With all the prosperity in the world they dwelt there together, the most famous knights under Christ and the loveliest ladies who ever lived, and he who held the court the most gracious of kings. For all these fair folk in the hall were in the prime of their age, the most
10 fortunate people under heaven, with a king whose spirits were the highest of all. It would be hard in our time to name so brave a company on any castle hill.

While the New Year was brisk because new come, the assembly on the daïs was served double portions when, after mass in the chapel had ended, the king with his knights came into the hall. Loud shouts arose from clerks and the others, who cried "Noel! Noel!" again and again. Forthwith the
20 nobles ran about to offer their gifts, demanding New Year's presents while they gave their own, and talking eagerly about the gifts. Ladies laughed aloud though they had lost in the exchange, and he who won was not displeased, you may well believe.

All this mirth they made until time for meat, when they washed suitably and went to their seats, the best man placed ever above, as was most seemly. In the midst of them the very lovely Guenevere was seated on the splendid daïs, surrounded by adorn-
30 ments. There were thin silk hangings all about her, while above rose a canopy of excellent cloth of Toulouse, with tapestries of Tharsia cloth which were embroidered and set with the finest gems that could be bought for any price at that day. She was most comely, and her grey eyes shone. No man

could say with truth that he ever saw anyone more fair.

But Arthur would not eat till all were served, he was so gay in his youth, and in a way so boyish. Life sat lightly upon him. He loved neither to lie long nor long to sit, so stirred within him his youthful blood and his restless brain. And another custom he had, too, which he had adopted in his magnificence: on such a high feast he would never
10 eat until there had been related to him a wonderful tale of something adventurous, of some great marvel that he could trust, of princes, of arms, of other great events; or until some trusty knight had besought him to joust and lay in peril dear life against life, each one the other, as fortune favored. This was the king's behavior at every feast that came, when he was in court among his noble household in the hall. Therefore with proud mien he stood boldly in his place on that New Year's Day, a very
20 valiant man. Much mirth he made withal.

Thus stood the brave king in his place before the high table, talking with courteous lightness. Good Gawain was placed beside Guenevere, and Agravain de la Dure Main sat on the other side, both of them sons of the king's sister and very trusty knights. Bishop Baldwin began the table above, and Iwain, Urien's son, ate with him. These were set on the daïs and splendidly served, and there were many brave knights besides at the side tables.
30 Then came the first course with the blaring of trumpets, which were hung with many bright banners. The sound of drums waked the echoes, with the tremulous notes of noble pipes, so that many a heart rose high at the sound. Full fair and dainty foods appeared therewith, abundance of fresh meats on so many plates that it was hard to find a place

on the cloth to set the silver dishes which held the
divers viands. Each man took ungrudged whatever
he pleased. Each pair had twelve dishes as well as
good beer and bright wine.

Now I will tell you no more of their service, for
every man can well understand that there was no
stinting. Another and different burst of sound came
thereupon, staying the knights from their repast,
for scarcely had the music ceased, and the first
10 course been properly served, when in at the hall
door came a terrible lord, one of the greatest and
tallest on earth. From his neck to his waist he was
so squarely built and so thick, and his loins and his
limbs were so long and so large, that he was half a
giant of earth, I believe, yet I declare him to have
been a man nevertheless, and the best formed for
one of his size who ever went riding forth. Although his body was thick in back and breast, his
belly and waist were becomingly slender, and all
20 parts of his body were clean-cut and shapely. Men
wondered at his color no less than at his form and
size. He bore himself like a valiant man and was
bright green all over.

The man and his garments were altogether green.
A straight narrow tunic clung to his body, with a
fair mantle over it lined with plain fur of a single
color, a brilliant and pleasant white, as was his hood
also, which was thrown back from his head and
laid on his shoulders. Neat well-fitting hose of the
30 same green encased his calves, and his bright golden
spurs were set on barred straps of rich silk, while
there were facings under his thighs to protect him
as he rode. All his clothing, indeed, was green,
even to the stripes of his belt and the bright gems
richly set against silken embroideries on his fair
garments and his saddle. It would be tedious to

tell half the designs that were worked in these embroideries—birds and insects of bright green mingled
with gold. The pendants of the steed's breast-trap-
pings, the magnificent crupper, the studs at the ends
of the bit, and all the metal work were enamelled
in the same fashion; the stirrups were of the one
hue, as likewise were the bows and noble skirts of
the saddle, which glimmered and gleamed with green
jewels. The horse he rode was gay with the same
10 color, you may be sure, a green steed large and
strong, with an embroidered bridle, difficult and
restive to manage but perfectly under the knight's
control.

Very gaily attired in green was the man, and the
hair of his head matched that of his horse. A
comely waving thatch of it covered his shoulders,
and over his breast fell a great beard like a bush,
which with the hair of his head hung down all
about above his elbows in such a way that half of
20 his arms were covered, just as a king's neck is
covered by his cape. The mane of the great horse
was much like the man's, well curled and combed,
with very many knots and with gold thread plaited
in the handsome green—ever a strand of the hair
and another of the gold. The tail and the forelock
were arranged in the same way, and both were tied
with a band of bright green, while the dock of the
tail was ornamented with very costly gems as well
as bound tight with a thong that had an intricate
30 knot at the top, on which tinkled many shining bells
of refined gold. Such a steed and such a rider
were never seen in that hall ere that time. He
looked, said all who saw him, as brilliant as lightning.
It seemed that no man could endure his blows.

Yet he had neither helmet nor hauberk, nor
gorget, nor any plate armor, nor spear to smite with,

nor shield for protection; but in one hand he carried a bunch of holly, which is greenest when the woods are bare, and in the other he bore a huge and monstrous axe, a cruel weapon, whoever might describe it. The head had the length of an ell, the spiked end was made of green steel and gold, and the bit was burnished bright, with a broad edge as keen as a sharp razor. It was fastened to a helve, the end of a strong staff, which was wound with
10 iron to the tip and chased with pleasant designs in green. A thong was wrapped about it, to which were attached both at the head and along the shaft, here and there, fine tassels set on richly embroidered buttons of bright green.

This knight came forward and entered the hall, making his way to the high daïs as if fearful of no danger. He greeted no one, but kept his eyes aloft. The first word he said was: "Where is the ruler of this company? Gladly would I see him and
20 hold speech with him." He cast his eyes over the knights, looking them up and down, then halted as if trying to see who was the most famous man in the hall.

There was prolonged scrutiny of the man, for everyone marvelled at the hue of the knight and his horse, as green as grass and greener, it seemed, glowing brighter than green enamel on gold. All who were standing about studied him and stepped nearer, wondering what in the world he was going
30 to do. Many wonders had the folk seen, but never before one such as this, on account of which they considered it illusion and magic. Many of the noble knights were thus afraid to answer, being altogether astonished at his voice, and sat stonestill in the dead silence that fell throughout the splendid hall. Their voices stopped at once, as if all had fallen

asleep—I think not wholly from fear, but partly from courtesy, in order to permit him whom all of them reverenced to address the man.

Then Arthur, as he beheld the strange thing happening before the high daïs, promptly saluted the knight, for he was never afraid. He said: "Welcome, indeed, sir knight, to this place. I am called Arthur and am the head of this house. Graciously dismount, I pray you, and what it is you wish we 10 shall learn hereafter."

"Nay," quoth the knight, "it is not my mission to remain any long while in this dwelling; but because your praise, my lord, is raised so high, and because your castle and your men are held the best in the world, and your knights the bravest who ride forth in steel armor, the strongest and most honorable of mankind, and valiant to sport with in all noble games, and because the chivalry here is famous, as I have heard, I have come hither at this time. You 20 may be certain by this holly bough which I bear that I come in peace and seek no quarrel, for had I set forth on this business in fighting wise, I have a hauberk at home and a helmet, too, a shield and a sharp spear shining bright, as well as other weapons to my hand, I assure you. But because I desired no protection, my equipment is less warlike. Only, if you are so brave as all men say, you will grant me by your grace the sport that I rightfully ask."

Arthur answered and said: "Courteous sir knight, 30 if you ask nothing more than battle, you shall not fail of a contest here."

"Nay, I ask for no fight, I tell you truly. There are only beardless children about this table here. If I were armed and set on a high steed, there is no man here to match me, their strength is so feeble. Therefore I am merely asking a Christmas game in

this court, for it is Yule and New Year's, and many
bold knights are here. If anyone in this castle holds
himself so brave, and is so valiant in mettle and so
reckless as to dare the exchange of one stroke for
another, I will give him this splendid battle-axe,
which is heavy enough, to handle as pleases him;
and I will suffer the first stroke unarmed as I sit
here. If any knight be so bold as to try what I
propose, let him come to me quickly and take the
10 weapon. I give him a quit-claim of it forever; he
may keep it as his own. I will accept unflinchingly
from him the blow as I stand. In recompense, you
will adjudge me the legal right to give him a stroke
in my turn, but grant him the respite of twelve
months and a day. Hasten now, and let us see
whether anyone here dare speak."

If he had astonished them at first, all the courtiers
in the hall were now even more quiet, both the
high and the low. The knight on the horse turned
20 and rolled his red eyes about fiercely, wrinkling
his bristling green eyebrows and sweeping his beard
from side to side, while he waited for someone to
rise.

When none would address him, he gave a loud
cough, cleared his throat resoundingly, and pro-
ceeded to speak. "Lo," quoth the knight, "is this
the house of Arthur, the fame of which runs through
so many kingdoms? Where now are your pride
and your conquests, your fierceness, your wrath,
30 and your boastful words? The gaiety and the glory
of the Round Table are destroyed by one man's
word, for all of you are cowering with fear before
a blow has been offered!"

Therewith he laughed so loud that Lord Arthur
grieved, and the blood rushed for shame into his
bright face. He grew as angry as the wind, as did

all who were there. The king, whose nature was
daring, approached the bold man, and said: "By
heaven, knight, what you ask is foolish, and it is
right for you to get what your folly demands. I
know of no man who is afraid of your bragging
words. Give me now your battle-axe, in God's
name, and I will grant the boon you ask."

Swiftly he stepped towards him and grasped at
his hand, while the other knight dismounted in proud
10 fashion. Now Arthur had the axe and, gripping
the helve, brandished it grimly, thinking to strike
with it. The bold man stood upright before him,
taller by a head and more than any other in the
hall. With serious face and unmoved countenance,
he stroked his beard and pulled down his tunic, no
more troubled or dismayed by the power of Arthur's
strokes than he would have been if someone were
bringing him wine to drink.

Gawain, from his place by the queen, bowed to
20 the king, saying: "Honored lord, I beg earnestly
that this affair may be mine. If you would bid
me come from this bench and stand by you there—
if I might without discourtesy and displeasure to
my liege lady leave the table—I would advise you
thus in the presence of your noble court. It seems
to me unseemly, if the truth be known, when such
a demand is made openly in your hall, that you
take it on yourself, capable though you be, when so
many brave men are sitting about you on the benches.
30 None is more warlike of spirit than they, I believe,
none stronger on the field of battle. I am the
feeblest of them, I know, and the weakest of understanding. To acknowledge the truth, the loss of my
life would matter least. Only inasmuch as you are
my uncle do I merit praise; no worth but your blood
have I in my body. Since this affair is so foolish

that it concerns you in no way, and since I have first asked to undertake it, turn it over to me. If I speak not what is right, blame not this honorable court."

The nobles took counsel together, and forthwith advised with one voice that the crowned king be released, and that the game be given to Gawain. Then the king commanded the knight to rise from his place; and he got up at once and approached
10 the king courteously, kneeling down before him and taking the weapon. The king graciously released it and with uplifted hand invoked God's blessing on Gawain, bidding him cheerfully to be strong in heart and hand.

"Take care, cousin," quoth the king, "how you manage the cut you give him. If you dispose of him well, I readily believe that you will be able to endure any blow he can offer afterwards!"

With the battle-axe in hand Gawain approached
20 the man, who awaited him boldly, in no wise dismayed.

Then the knight in green spoke to Sir Gawain. "Let us rehearse our agreement before we go further. First, knight, I beg that you will tell me your name truly."

"On my honor," quoth the good knight, "I am called Gawain. I will give you this blow, irrespective of what may befall hereafter; and a twelve-month hence I will take another from you with what-
30 ever weapon you please, but from no other man alive."

The other answered: "Sir Gawain, on my life I am wondrously glad that you are to give the stroke. By God," went on the green knight, "it pleases me that I am to receive at your hand what I have sought here. You have fully and properly rehearsed in

very correct form all the covenant that I asked of
the king, save that you shall assure me, sir, on your
honor, that you will seek me out yourself wherever
on earth you believe I may be found, and receive
payment in kind for what you give me to-day before
this noble company."

"Where shall I find you?" quoth Gawain. "Where
is your dwelling? By Him Who made me, I know
not where you live, and I know not you, sir knight
10 —neither your court nor your name. Instruct me
rightly, and tell me by what name you are called, and
I will use all my power to win thither; and that I
swear to you in truth by my honor."

"That is enough at New Year's," quoth the man
in green to gracious Gawain. "Nothing more is
necessary. If, indeed, after I have received the
buffet and you have given me your skilful stroke,
I tell you at once my house, my home, and my name,
then you may seek me out and fulfil your agreement;
20 and if I do not speak, then you shall speed the better. for you may remain in your land and inquire
no further. But stay! Take your grim weapon,
and let us see how you give a blow."

"Gladly, sir," quoth Gawain. He stroked his axe.
The green knight promptly took his stand with his
head a little bowed to uncover the bare flesh. He
drew his splendid long locks up over his head and
exposed his neck for the business in hand. Gawain,
setting his left foot forward, gripped his axe and
30 raised it aloft, then let it fall swiftly on the neck.
The edge clove the bones of the man, going through
the bright flesh and cutting it asunder, and the shining steel blade pierced the ground. The fair head
fell from the neck to the earth, so that many thrust
at it with their feet as it rolled away. Blood spurted
from the body and showed bright against the green.

Nevertheless the man neither faltered nor fell; but started forth vigorously on sturdy legs, groped about in a terrible way where people were standing, clutched his fair head, and lifted it up. Then he turned to his steed, caught the bridle, put his foot into the stirrup, and swung aloft, holding the head in his hand by the hair. Though he was headless, he sat as firmly in the saddle as if no mishap had befallen him. The ugly bleeding body turned the
10 horse about. Many a man had fear of him by the time his speech was ended.

For he held up the head in his hand, turning the face towards the most noble lady on the daïs; and it lifted up its eyelids and gazed with eyes wide open, and spoke as you may hear. "See that you be ready to go as you have promised, Sir Gawain; and search loyally until you find me, as you have promised in the hearing of these knights. Go to the Green Chapel, I charge you, to receive a blow like the one
20 you have given—as you merit—which will be promptly delivered on New Year's morn. Many men know me as the Knight of the Green Chapel. Therefore you will not fail to find me if you make the quest. So come, or you will deserve to be called recreant."

With a fierce roar he tightened the reins and, holding the head in his hands, passed out of the hall door so quickly that sparks flew from the hooves of his steed. To what race he belonged none there
30 knew, any more than they could tell whence he had come. What of that? The king and Gawain smiled and laughed aloud at the green knight. Yet it was accounted wholly a marvel among those men.

Although gracious King Arthur wondered in his heart, he let no such impression be seen, but said aloud to the beautiful queen with courteous words:

"Dear lady, do not be troubled at all to-day. Such affairs are well suited to Christmas, with playing of interludes, and laughter and song and the courtly dancing of carols by knights and ladies. Nevertheless, I may well sit down to my meat, for I cannot deny that I have seen a marvel." He glanced at Gawain, and said courteously: "Now, sir, hang up your axe, which has hewed enough."

And it was placed above the daïs, hanging against 10 the tapestry at the back, where all men might see and marvel at it, accounting it truly a wonder. Then the two lords, the king and the good knight, sat down at the table, and brave men served them double portions of whatever was best. With all manner of feasting and minstrelsy they passed the day happily till it came to an end. Now take heed, Sir Gawain, and do not try because of the danger to avoid this adventure you have taken in hand.

II

This handsel of adventures had Arthur at the 20 New Year, because he was eager to hear of bold undertakings. Although there was lack of vaunting words when they sat down, they were now well provided with serious business, their hands over-full of it. Gawain was glad when he began the game in the hall; but do not be surprised though the end be grievous. For though men are merry when they have taken strong drink, a year runs very quickly and never brings back what has passed. The end is very seldom like the beginning.

30 So this Yule went by, and the year thereafter, and one season followed another in due course. After Christmas came crabbed Lent which tries the flesh with fish and simpler food. But then the weather

contends with winter. The cold shrinks away, clouds rise, bright falls the rain on the fair meadows in warm showers, flowers appear. Both earth and forest are clothed in green. Birds prepare to build and sing bravely from delight in the soft summer which is coming on the hill-slopes; and blossoms swell to their bloom in the richly luxuriant hedge-rows, while splendid song is heard in the proud wood. Afterward comes summer with its soft breezes, when Zephyr blows gently over seedlings and herbs. Very lovely is the plant that grows up while the dampening dew drips from the leaves, awaiting the happy gleam of the bright sun. But then follows autumn apace, hardens the plant, and warns it to come to full ripeness ere winter. Autumn stirs the dust to rise with drought, flying high above the face of earth. Fierce winds of heaven wrestle with the sun, the leaves drop from the trees and light on the ground, and the grass fades that erstwhile was green. Then all that has grown up ripens and decays.

Thus runs the year away into many yesterdays, and winter returns again, as in truth is the way of the world. The Michaelmas moon came with its pledge of winter. Then Gawain thought full soon of his troublesome journey.

Yet until Allhallows' Day he remained with Arthur, who made an entertainment for the knight's sake on that feast, a great and splendid revel of the Round Table. Full courteous knights and lovely ladies were grieving on account of the prince; but none the less they were ready of speech and mirthful. Many who were sorrowful on the gentle knight,s behalf made their jests there.

After the feasting he spoke soberly to his uncle about his journey, and without pretence said thus:

"Liege lord of my life, I beg permission to leave you.
You know the nature of this matter: I need by no
means tell you the trouble of it. But I am bound
without fail to start forth to-morrow for the blow,
to seek the green man as God may guide me."

Then the noblest in the castle assembled, Iwain,
and Eric, and full many others: Sir Dodinal de
Sauvage, the Duke of Clarence, Lancelot, Lionel,
and good Lucan, Sir Boor and Sir Bedivere, both
10 strong men, Sir Mador de la Port, and many another
honorable knight. All this courtly company approached the king with sorrowful hearts to give
counsel to the knight. There was much lamentation
in the hall that one so honored as Gawain should go
on that errand, to endure a grievous blow and make
no return with his sword.

The knight made good cheer throughout, and said:
"Why should I hesitate? What may a man do but
go to meet his fate, however harsh and terrible?"
20 All that day he remained there, and in the morning made ready. He asked for his arms early, and
they were all brought. First a carpet of red Toulouse was spread on the floor, and much gilded gear
glittered upon it. The brave man stepped thereon
and fingered the steel. He was dressed in a doublet
of fine Tharsia cloth, with a well-cut cape, short and
full and fastened together at the neck, which was
trimmed inside with brilliant white fur. Then they
put sabatouns on the knight's feet, and enclosed his
30 legs in splendid greaves of steel with polished knee-
pieces attached thereto, which were tied about his
knees with gold knots. Goodly cuisses, which skilfully protected his sturdy thighs, were fastened on
with thongs. The knight was then enfolded in a
linked corslet of bright steel rings, with a backing of
noble cloth. There were well-burnished arm-pieces,

and elbow-guards strong and bright, and gloves of plate, and all the fine gear that could serve him: a gorgeous coat-armor, gold spurs splendidly fastened, and a very trusty sword belted on with a girdle of silk. When he was clasped in his arms, his harness was rich indeed. The least latchet and loop gleamed with gold.

Dressed as he was, he heard mass, which was offered and celebrated at the high altar. Then he
10 came to the king and to his companions of the court, and graciously took leave of the lords and ladies; and they kissed him and escorted him forth, commending him to Christ.

By that time Gringolet was ready, girded with a saddle that gleamed very bright with many gold fringes and in preparation for the adventure was newly studded with nails. The bridle was striped transversely and bound with bright gold; the ornamentation of the breastpiece and of the superb sad-
20 dle-skirts, the crupper, and the horsecloth matched the saddle-bows; and all were red, studded with rich gold nails which glittered and glinted like the gleaming sun.

Then the knight took his helmet and quickly kissed it. It was stoutly stapled and padded within, set high on his head, and fastened behind. Over the beaver was a light covering, which was embroidered and adorned with the finest gems on a broad silken hem, with birds on the seams, parrots preening at
30 intervals, turtle-doves and true-love knots set so thickly that it seemed many a damsel must have been seven winters at work upon it. The circlet that surrounded the crown of the helmet was even more precious, a device of bright and shining diamonds.

Then they brought to him his shield, which was of bright gules, with a pentangle depicted upon it.

in pure gold. Taking it by the baldric, the knight put
it about his neck, and it became him most excellently.
Why the pentangle belonged to this noble prince I
must tell you, even though it delay me. It is a symbol that Solomon once devised to betoken truth, as
can be seen from the description; for it is a figure
having five points, and each line overlaps and locks
in another, and everywhere it is endless. The English always term it, as I hear, the endless knot.
10 Therefore it suited this knight and his bright arms,
for ever faithful in five ways, and five times in
each way, was Gawain known to be; and like refined
gold he was free from all unchivalrous qualities as
well as graced with virtues at court. On this account
he bore the new pentangle in his shield and coat-
armor, as a man accounted most true and as a knight
most gentle of conduct.

First, he was found faultless in his five wits; and
again, the man never failed with his five fingers; and
20 all his trust in the world was in the five wounds
which Christ received on the cross, as the creed tells
us. And wheresoever he was fighting, he steadfastly
kept in mind, no matter what occurred, that all his
pride must be in the five joys which the gracious
Queen of Heaven got of her Child. For this reason the knight had her image beautifully depicted
in the upper half of his shield, so that when he
looked thereto his courage never failed. The fifth
five that the man showed, as I find, were generosity
30 and love of his fellow men more than all things
else, purity and courtesy that never wavered, and
pity, which surpasses all points. These noble five
were more firmly attached to this knight than to
any other. With all of them he was, in truth, five
times girt about; and each one was joined to another
so that they had no end; and they were fixed upon

five points which never failed, neither gathering together on one side nor sundering, being without an end at any angle, wherever one started or finished. Therefore the figure was fashioned royally on his bright shield with red gold on red gules. This is what learned men call the true pentangle.

Now was fair Gawain ready. He took his spear straightway, and bade them all farewell—forevermore, as he thought. Then he struck the steed with
10 his spurs and hastened forth so fast that sparks flew from the stones as he rode away. All who saw the comely knight sighed in their hearts and said, indeed, each to the other, grieving for him: "By Christ, it is wrong that you, my lord, who are noble of life, should be so lost! To find his equal on earth, in faith, is not easy. To have wrought more carefully would have been more sensible. It would have been better to make yonder noble knight a duke, for he would have been a brilliant leader
20 in war; and that would have befitted him better than to be destroyed for naught, beheaded by a monster for the vanity of pride. Who ever heard of any king's so sacrificing his knights for the sport of Christmas games!" Many tears fell from their eyes when the noble lord went from the court that day. He stopped not, but sturdily went forward. Many a bewildering path he rode, as the story tells us.

Now rode Sir Gawain, as God willed, through the realm of Logres, though it brought him no pleasure.
30 Often companionless and alone he stayed at night in places where his fare was by no means to his liking. He had no comrade but his steed through forests and across downs, no being but God to speak with by the way, until he came near to North Wales. All the islands of Anglesey he kept on his left hand, and passed over the fords by the headlands of Holy

Head, coming to shore in the Forest of Wirral. But few dwelt there who loved either God or man with good heart. And ever he inquired, as he journeyed, from the men he met, if they had heard of a green knight in any place thereabout, or of the Green Chapel. All denied that ever in their lives they had seen a man of such a green hue. The knight took strange roads on many a dreary hillside. His mood changed often ere he found that chapel.

10   Many cliffs he scrambled over in strange regions, and rode as an alien far removed from his friends. At each riverside or ford where he passed, he found an enemy before him, as a rule: a foe so evil and so fierce that he had to fight. The knight encountered so many marvels among the hills that it would be tedious to tell the tenth part of them. Sometimes he warred with dragons, and with wolves, too; sometimes with forest creatures that dwelt in the rocks; with wild bulls, with bears, and with boars
20 at other times; and with giants who pursued him from the high fells. Had he not been doughty and steadfast, and served the Lord, he would surely have been slain full often. For troublesome as the fighting was, the winter weather was worse, when the clear cold rain fell from the clouds and froze ere it touched the sere earth. Almost dead with the sleet, he slept in his armor more nights than enough, where the cold stream ran clattering from the mountain-top and hung in hard icicles above his head.
30 Thus in peril and distress and hardship the knight journeyed alone through the country till Christmas Eve. At that tide he made his petition to Mary that she would direct his course and guide him to some habitation.

In the morning he rode pleasantly along a mountain slope into a very deep and wild forest, which was flanked by high hills on each side. There were clumps of hoary oaks, a hundred together, and tangles of hazel and hawthorn everywhere clothed with rough ragged moss. On the bare twigs many unhappy birds, distressed by the cold, piped sorrowfully. The knight on Gringolet went on beneath the trees through many a bog and swamp, all by himself, troubled about his religious duties, lest he should not be able to attend a service to the Lord, Who on 10 that same night was born of a virgin to end our sorrow.

Therefore he said, sighing: "I beseech Thee, Lord, and Mary Thy dearest and gentlest mother, for some lodging where I may hear mass solemnly, and Thy matins to-morrow. I ask this meekly, and to that end I pray forthwith my Pater Noster and Ave and Creed." While he prayed, he rode on, confessing his misdeeds, and crossed himself repeatedly, saying: "The Cross of Christ aid me!"

20 He had crossed himself but thrice when he became aware on a hill above a glade of a moated dwelling, framed in by the boughs of many great trees which grew along the moat: the most lovely castle that ever knight owned, set on a meadow, with a park all about surrounded by a spiked palisade that enclosed the trees for more than two miles. The knight viewed the stronghold as it shimmered and shone through the bright oaks, then reverently took off his helmet and solemnly thanked Jesus and 30 St. Julian, who in their gentleness had shown courtesy to him and hearkened to his cry. "Now," quoth the man, "I beseech you yet for good lodging!" Then he spurred Gringolet with his gilt heels, and by good fortune found the main road that brought him speedily to the bridge end. The bridge was drawn up securely, the gates were shut fast; the

walls were strongly fashioned. No blast of the winds had it need to fear.

The knight waited on his steed by the bank of the deep double moat that surrounded the place. The walls plunged marvellously deep into the water and rose aloft to a very great height, all of solid hewn stone up to the cornice with its horn-works under the battlement. Above were fair watch-towers, provided at intervals with many fine loop-holes that
10 fastened securely. The knight had never looked upon better outworks; and within he beheld a very lofty hall, as well as many turreted towers and beautiful high pinnacles with skilfully carved and ornamented summits. He saw many chalk-white chimneys that gleamed on the tower roofs. So many pointed pinnacles were scattered everywhere, clustered so thickly about the embrasures of the battlements, that the castle seemed cut out of paper.

The nobleman on his steed thought it very fair,
20 if only he might enter the refuge and find lodging there while the holy day lasted that was at hand. He called, and soon a very civil porter, coming out on the wall to know his errand, hailed the errant knight.

"Good sir," quoth Gawain, "will you take a message from me to the high lord of this house, to beg lodgement?"

"Yea, by Peter," quoth the porter, "but indeed I am sure, sir knight, that you are welcome to dwell
30 here while you please."

Quickly the man returned with other folk to give the knight courteous reception. They let down the great drawbridge and, coming out, knelt down on the cold earth to welcome him as seemed honorable to them. As they had set the broad gates wide open for him, he bade them at once to rise, and rode

over the bridge. Several equerries assisted him to
dismount, and then brave men led his steed to stable.
Knights and squires came down to convey him joyfully into the hall. When he lifted up his helmet,
there were many to serve him and receive it at his
hands; and they took from him both his sword and
his shield. He greeted each of the proud nobles
graciously, as they pressed forward to do him honor.
Still dressed in his splendid armor, they took him
into the hall, where a delightful fire burned proudly
on the floor.

The lord of the people came forth from his chamber to greet the visitor with honor. He said: "You
are welcome to rule as you like all that is here.
Everything is yours, to have and to hold at your
will."

"Many thanks," quoth Gawain. "May Christ reward you!"

The knights embraced with seeming gladness.
Gawain looked at the man who had greeted him so
courteously, and thought the owner of the castle a
brave knight, a huge one, too, and in the prime of
life. Stalwart was he, and his beard was reddish
brown; stern was he, and he stood firm on his sturdy
legs. His countenance was as terrifying as fire,
though in speech he was courteous. It seemed to
Gawain that he was well fitted to hold rule over good
lieges.

The lord turned to a chamber, bidding them
assign people quickly to serve the guest with defer-
ence. At the command, men enough were ready,
who brought him to a bright chamber, where the
bedding was splendid: the sheets of pure silk
hemmed with bright gold, the coverlets very elaborate, with beautiful panels of brilliant white fur
and embroidered besides, the curtains sliding on

cords with red gold rings. On the walls were hangings of Toulouse cloth and Tharsia silk, and similar
tapestries under foot on the floor. There the knight
was relieved of his corslet and the rest of his bright
armor. Men quickly brought him rich robes to
wear at his choice. As soon as he took one and
donned it, it became him well with its spreading
folds. Almost like the springtime he appeared to
every man in his varied colors, with all his limbs
10 beneath glowing and delightful. It seemed to them
that Christ never made a more comely knight. No
matter where he might go through the world, he
would be a prince without a peer on any field of
battle.

A chair with coverings and quilted cushions, both
cunningly made, was pleasantly arranged for Sir
Gawain before the hearth, where burned a fire of
charcoal. And then there was thrown over him a
beautiful mantle of bright silk, richly embroidered
20 and furred within with the best skins trimmed with
ermine, as was also the hood. So he sat in the
splendid chair and warmed himself until his frame
of mind grew more cheerful.

Soon a table was set up on trestles very fairly,
covered with a clean cloth of pure white, with an
over-cloth, a salt-cellar, and silver spoons. The
knight washed at his good pleasure and began to eat.
Men served him in seemly fashion with various excellent broths, admirably seasoned, double portions
30 as was right; and many kinds of fish, some baked
in bread, some broiled on the coals, some boiled,
some in stews flavored with spices, and all with such
well-made sauces that the hero was pleased. Often
with courtesy and graciousness he called it a feast
indeed, though the knights, as was good manners,
encouraged him to eat by saying: "Accept this peni-

tential fare. Later it shall be bettered." The knight grew mirthful as the wine went to his head.

Then by discreet and tactful questions they made inquiry of the prince, until he courteously acknowledged that he came from the court held by noble and gracious Arthur, the splendid royal king of the Round Table, and that he was Gawain himself sitting there, come, as chance befell, to that Christmas celebration.

When the lord heard that he had the knight as guest, he laughed aloud at the news, so pleased was he; and all men in the company were happy that they were soon to be in the presence of one to whom belonged all excellence and valor and courtly manners, a man ever praised and honored beyond all others on earth. Each knight said to his comrade: "Now shall we see courtesy well exemplified, and hear noble speech without reproach. We may learn without asking what conversation ought to be, since we have caught the fine father of good breeding. God has surely been gracious to us in granting us such a guest as Gawain at this time when men sit and sing of Christ's birth. This man shall instruct us in noble manners, and those who hear him shall learn the art of lovers' dalliance."

By the time dinner was at an end and the noble visitor had risen, it was nearly night. Chaplains went to the chapel and rang very loudly, as was proper, for the devout evensong of the high festival. The lord went thither, and his lady gracefully entered her closed pew. Gawain hastened in happy mood and followed them. The lord took him by a fold of his mantle and led him to a seat, calling him familiarly by name and saying that he was most welcome of all men in the world. Gawain thanked

him hastily, and they embraced and sat soberly one
by the other throughout the service.

Then the lady wished to look upon the knight,
and came forth from her closet with many lovely
maidens. She was the fairest of them all in the
texture of her neck and face, in her color, her figure,
and her gentle ways—more beautiful than Guenevere,
as it seemed to the knight. He went through the
chancel to salute the gracious lady courteously. At
10 her left hand she was attended by another lady
who was older than she, an ancient dame highly
honored by the company of knights. Unlike to look
on were those ladies, for if one was young and fresh,
withered was the other. Rich red mantled the
cheeks of the one, while the rough and wrinkled
cheeks of the other hung in loose folds. The head-
dress of the one, ornamented with many gleaming
pearls, left bare her breast and white throat, which
shone brighter than snow new fallen on the hills;
20 the other's neck was covered with a gorget, her
black chin bound up with a white veil, her forehead
hidden by silk, and she was muffled up everywhere,
turreted and tricked out with ornaments, so that
nothing was visible of the lady but her black eyebrows, the two eyes, the nose, the bare lips, and
those were unpleasant to see and strangely bleared.
One may call her, before God, a worshipful lady!
Her body was short and thick, with broad and
rounded hips. Sweeter to look upon was the lady
30 she led!

When Gawain saw the fair lady, who surveyed
him graciously, he went up to the two with permission of the lord, saluted the elder with a low bow,
but lightly embraced the more lovely, and kissed
her in seemly fashion, while he spoke as a knight
should do. They received him in a friendly way,

and he quickly asked that if it pleased them they
would accept him as their servant. They took him
between them and led him, as they talked, to the
hearth in the chamber, where they called for spices
and good wine, which men hastened to bring them
in profusion. The lord often sprang from his seat,
urging them many times over to be merry. Gaily
he pulled off his hood and hung it on a spear,
offering the honorable possession of it to the one
10 who made the most mirth during Christmas. "And
I shall try, by my faith, if my friends will help,
to contend with the best, before I lose my hood."
Thus the lord made merry, to gladden Sir Gawain
that night with sport in the hall, until the time came
when he called for a light. Sir Gawain took leave
and went to his bed.

On the morning which recalls to every man the
time when the Lord was born to die for us, happiness comes to each dwelling in the world for His
20 sake. So did it there on that day with many de-
lights. Cunningly made dishes were served on the
daïs by stout retainers. The ancient dame sat in the
highest place, with the lord courteously leaning
towards her. Gawain and the fair lady sat together in places of equal honor, as the service duly
began. And afterward throughout the hall, in a
way to please them, each man was promptly served
according to his degree. There was meat, there was
mirth, there was so much joy that to recount it all
30 would be hard for me if peradventure I tried to
describe it in detail. Yet I know that Gawain and
the beautiful lady had so much pleasure of each
other's company in their private dalliance, the pure
and virtuous courtesy of their talk, that their play
truly surpassed the enjoyment of the other nobles.
Each man minded his sport, and those two minded

theirs, while trumpets and drums and pipes sounded about them.

Much joy there was on that day and the next; and the third was equally filled with delight, for the merriment of St. John's Day was pleasant to hear. That was the last of the entertainment, they thought, and the guests were to depart at the gray dawn thereafter. So they held high revel and drank wine, dancing unceasingly in joyous carols. At 10 last, when it was late, they took their leave, each strong man to wend his way on the morrow. As Gawain bade farewell, the good lord held him back and led him to the chimney-place in his own chamber. There in privacy he thanked him warmly for the honor he had done to him and his house at that high festival, by adorning the castle with his gracious presence.

"Indeed, sir, while I live, I shall fare the better because Gawain has been my guest at God's own 20 feast."

"Many thanks, sir," quoth Gawain, "All the honor is your own, in good faith. The High King reward you! I am your man, as I rightly should be, to work your will in high things and low."

The lord insistently tried to keep the knight longer, but Gawain answered that he could by no means stay. Then the lord asked him very courteously what serious business had driven him to journey all alone from the king's court so daringly at that time 30 of the year, before the holidays were past.

"Truly, sir," quoth the knight, "you say but the truth. A high and pressing errand took me from court, for I am summoned to a place that I know not how to seek for, or whither in the world to go to find it. For all the land in Logres I would not fail to come to it on New Year's morning, so our Lord help me! Therefore, sir, I make this request of you here, that you tell me truly if ever you have heard any tale of the Green Chapel and where it stands, or of the Green Knight who holds it. A solemn agreement was made between us that I should meet the man there if I lived. It now wants but little of the New Year; and, by God's Son, I would see the man more gladly, if God would permit, than have any other blessing whatsoever. I 10 have now barely three days, and I would as gladly fall dead as fail of my mission."

Then, laughing, the lord said: "It is better for you to stay on, for I can direct you to the place where the Green Chapel stands by the end of the time you have set. Grieve no more. You shall remain at your ease in your bed here while the days pass, and set forth on the first of the year, yet reach your goal by mid-morning, to do what pleases you there. Dwell here until New Year's Day, then 20 rise and go. You shall be set on your way. It is but two miles hence."

Then Gawain was very glad, and laughed merrily. "I thank you heartily above all else. Since my adventure is achieved, I shall stay at your will and do whatever you judge best."

At this the lord placed him by his side, had the ladies fetched for their greater delight, and in this privacy they took their pleasure together. The lord in his high spirits made merry speeches like a man 30 who had lost his wits and knew not what he did.

He cried out to the knight: "You have agreed to do whatever I bid. Will you hold to the promise here and now?"

"Yea, forsooth, sir," said the loyal man, "while I remain in your castle, I will be obedient to your command."

"You have travelled from afar," quoth the lord, "and because you have revelled with me since, you are not well recovered either in food or sleep, as I know of a truth. You shall stay in your upper room and lie at your ease to-morrow morning until time for mass, and go to meat when you will with my wife, who will sit with you and give the pleasure of her company till I return to court. Remain you here, and I shall rise early and go 10 hunting."

Gawain agreed to all this, bowing courteously.

"Yet further," quoth the lord, "we shall make a covenant. Whatsoever I get in the forest shall be yours, and whatever fortune you win give it to me in exchange. Swear on your honor, dear lord, to make this exchange, whether worse come or better."

"By God," quoth the noble Gawain, "I agree thereto, and I am glad it pleases you to make this sport." 20 Said the lord of the castle: "The bargain is made. Who brings us drink to seal it?"

They laughed and drank, trifling and exchanging badinage, these lords and ladies, while it pleased them. And afterward with Gallic courtesy and many fine words they rose and stood for a little, speaking quietly, then kissed one another graciously and separated. With many deft attendants and gleaming torches each man was brought to his bed at last in comfort. Yet ere they went to bed, they 30 often rehearsed their covenant. The old lord of the people knew well how to keep a game in hand.

III

Full early before dawn the folk arose; and those guests who were leaving called their servants, who

hastened to saddle the horses, prepare their gear, and pack their bags. The nobles, all arrayed for riding, made ready, mounted lightly, and took their bridles, each man on the way he pleased. The noble lord of the land with his retinue of knights was not the last one ready to depart. When he had heard mass, he ate a morsel of food hastily, and with a bugle-call hastened swiftly to the hunting-field. As soon as daylight dawned upon earth, he and his
10 knights were on their tall steeds.

Then the well-trained dog-grooms coupled their hounds, opened the kennel door, and called them out, blowing loudly three single notes on their bugles. The hounds bayed at the sound and made a brave noise. A hundred huntsmen of the best whipped in and turned back the ones that strayed away. The keepers went to their stations, and the huntsmen unleashed the hounds. There rose in the forest the great tumult of bugle blasts.

20 At the first cry of the hounds, the wild deer trembled, rushed through the valley in their terror, and away to the hills; but they were promptly stopped by the cordon of shouting beaters. The beaters let the harts with the tall heads pass by, and the brave bucks, too, with the broad palms on their antlers; for the noble lord had forbidden anyone to touch the male deer in the close season. The hinds were held within the circle by cries of "hay!" and "ware!", the does driven back with a great
30 noise to the deep valley. There one could see, as they passed, the rushing flight of arrows; at each turn in the wood sped an arrow, which mightily pierced a shining hide with its broad head. Lo! they cried out, they bled, they died on the hillslopes. All the while, the racing hounds tore after them swiftly, and the hunters with loud horns hastened

on with such a ringing cry as if the cliffs had burst
asunder. Whatever game escaped the men who
were shooting was pulled down and slain at the
receiving stations, after the beasts had been driven
from the heights and down to the waters. The men
at the lower stations were skilled, and the greyhounds so powerful that they seized them at once
and pulled them down straightway, as fast as men
could look. The lord, enraptured, rushed in again
10 and again, and dismounted, passing the day joyously in this manner till came the dark night.

While the lord was making sport on the edge of
the forest, good Gawain lay in his magnificent bed.
idling until daylight gleamed on the walls, under
bright covers and curtained about. As he was
quietly dozing, he heard a slight noise cautiously
made at his door, and heard it quickly open. He
lifted his head out of the clothes, raised a corner
of the curtain a little, and looked warily to see what
20 it might be.

It was the lady, most beautiful to behold, who
closed the door after her very quietly and moved
towards the bed. The knight in embarrassment
lay down, and craftily pretended to be asleep. She
stole in silence to his bed, lifted the curtain, and
crept inside, where she sat down gently on the
edge of the bed and stayed there, waiting for him
to awake. He lay quiet for a long while and pon-
dered on the possible results of the affair. It seemed
30 to him very strange, yet he said to himself: "It would
be more courteous of me to find out as soon as may
be what she wishes." Rousing himself and stirring, he turned towards her and opened his eyes,
then pretended to be astonished and made the sign
of the cross, as if to protect himself. With the
white and red blended in her face, she began to

speak most graciously, and on her delicate lips was
a smile.

"Good-morrow, Sir Gawain," said the fair lady.
"You are a careless sleeper to allow anyone to steal
in like this. Now that you are caught, I shall im-
prison you in bed, you may be sure, unless we come
to terms." Laughingly the lady uttered the jest.

"Good-morrow, fair one," quoth the merry Gawain, "I am in your power, and that pleases me
10 well, for I yield at once and beg for mercy, which
is best, I am sure, since I can do nothing else."
Thus he turned the jest with a happy laugh. "But
if you would give me leave, lovely lady, by releas-
ing your prisoner and asking him to rise, I would
remove myself from this bed and array myself
more suitably. I should have the more comfort in
talking with you."

"Nay, forsooth," said the sweet lady, "you shall
not rise from your bed, I assure you. I shall keep
20 you here and talk with my knight whom I have
captured. For I know very well you are that
Gawain whom all the world honors, wherever you
journey. Your honor and courtesy are praised by
lords and ladies—by every living creature. And
now you are here, to be sure, and we are alone. My
lord and his train have gone afield; other men are
in their beds, as are my ladies; the door is closed
and securely fastened. Since I have the favorite
of everyone here in the house, I shall use my time
30 well in conversation while it lasts. You are welcome
to my body to do with it what you will. I ought to
serve you, and so I shall do."

"On my honor," quoth Gawain, "though I am
not the man you picture me, I seem to profit by it.
I know well that I am unworthy of such honor as
you mention; but I should be glad, by God, if you

permitted, to have the joy of pleasing you in word or deed. That would rejoice me."

"In good faith, Sir Gawain," quoth the lovely lady, "if I found fault with the excellence and prowess that please all others, or held them lightly, I should fail in courtesy. There are plenty of ladies who would rather have you in their power, gracious knight, as I have you here, to enjoy the dalliance of your charming speeches and to get comfort and
10 relief from their sorrows, than all the treasure and gold they possess. But I praise the Lord of Heaven that through His grace I have what all desire."

Very gracious was the fair lady, but the knight replied discreetly to everything she chanced to say. "Madam," quoth the courteous man, "Mary reward you! Your generosity, in very truth, is noble. People most commonly take their line of conduct from others, and they foolishly exaggerate the courtesy they pay me. In reality, I am to be valued
20 only on account of the honor you pay me, because you cannot go wrong."

"By Mary," quoth the lady, "it seems otherwise to me. If I were equal to all the women alive, and had the entire wealth of the world in my possession, and if I were to bargain for the choice of a lord, no knight on earth should be selected before you, sir, both on account of your manners that I have observed, your beauty, your courtesy, and your happy demeanor—what I knew by report earlier
30 and now find to be true."

"You might certainly choose much better, dear lady," quoth the knight, "but I am proud of the praise you give me, and as your true servant I hold you my sovereign, and make myself your knight. May Christ reward you!"

Thus they talked of many things until morning

passed, and ever the lady made it appear that she loved him greatly, while the knight was on the defence, but acted very courteously. "Though I were the most beautiful of ladies," the lady thought to herself, "he would show me no love." It was because of the terrible event he was soon to meet, the unavoidable blow that would strike him down.

The lady then spoke of departure, and he did not restrain her. She said good-bye with a laugh-
10 ing glance, but amazed him by the gibe she gave as she lingered: "May He Who gives us speech reward you for this entertainment! But that you are Gawain I am inclined to disbelieve."

"Why?" asked the knight, and repeated the question, fearful lest he had been at fault in the manner of his speeches.

The lady blessed him, and said as follows: "Anyone so courteous as Gawain is held to be—and that is pure courtesy itself—could not well have been
20 so long with a lady without begging her for a kiss, out of politeness and by some trifling hint, at least, at the end of some speech or other."

Then said Gawain: "Let it be as you will, to be sure. I shall kiss you at your command, as a knight should, and go further to avoid your displeasure. So plead no more."

She approached at that and caught him in her arms, bending down and kissing him. Thereupon they commended each other to Christ, and she left
30 the room without further speech.

He prepared hurriedly to rise, called to his chamberlain, selected his garments, and when he was ready went forth to mass. Then he passed on to the meal which awaited him, and made merry all day till the rising of the moon. A knight was never more fairly placed between two ladies of such worth

as the older and the younger. Much pleasure they
had together.

And ever the lord of the land continued at his
sport, hunting the barren hinds in forest and heath.
A marvellous number of does and other deer he
killed while daylight lasted. Then at length the folk
assembled proudly and made a quarry of the slain
deer. The nobles came thither with their attendants,
selected the fattest of the beasts, and ceremoniously
10 cut them open, as custom demands. Certain ones
made the assay, and found two fingers of fat on
the poorest of them.

Then they made a slit above the breastbone, seized
the first stomach, cut it open with a sharp knife, and
tied it up. Next they slashed the four legs and
stripped off the hide, then broke open the belly and
took out the bowels, cunningly removing also the
flesh of the knot in the flanks. Gripping the throat,
they carefully separated the gullet from the wind-
20 pipe and took out the lungs. Then they cut out
the shoulders with sharp knives, slitting round
them along a narrow passage in order to keep the
sides uninjured. Next they broke up the breast,
separating it, and, beginning at the throat, ripped
it quickly to the fork of the legs, taking out the
advancers. After that they cut the membranes along
the ribs, and stripped off the hide along the backbone straight down to the haunches, so that it all
hung together and could be lifted as a whole and
30 cut off. This they took for the numbles, as I
believe they are called. At the forks of the thighs
they cut the loose folds of skin from behind, and
quickly cut the forks in two, to separate them from
the backbone. Then they cut off the head and neck,
and split the sides along the backbone, throw-
ing the ravens' fee of gristle into the branches of a

tree. Next they pierced each thick side through by the ribs, and hung them up by the hocks of the legs, each man to have his portion as is the custom. On one of the deerskins they fed their hounds with liver, lights, and tripe, mixed with bread soaked in blood.

Bravely they blew the signal call of capture, while the hounds bayed. Then they took their venison and turned towards home, sounding loud many a 10 note on their horns. By the time daylight had gone, the whole company had returned to the fair castle, where the knight had remained without stirring. Joyously the lord came in where the bright fire was kindled, and greeted Gawain with delight.

Then the lord commanded all the household to assemble in the hall, and bade call both the ladies down with their maidens. In sight of all the folk he told his men to fetch his venison, and called out to Gawain in high glee, showing him the tally of 20 nimble beasts and pointing out the bright fat on the ribs.

"How like you this sport? Have I won your praise? Have I deserved your hearty thanks by my skill?"

"Indeed, yes," quoth the other man, "here is the finest hunting I have seen these seven years in the winter season."

"And I give you all, Gawain," said the lord, "for by our covenant you may claim it as your own."
30 "That is true," quoth the knight. "I say the same to you. What I have honorably won in this house is certainly yours with equally good will." He clasped the lord's fair neck in his arms and kissed him as courteously as he knew how. "There you have my winnings. I achieved nothing more;

but if there had been more, I would give it to you completely."

"Many thanks," quoth the good man. "It is good, yet perhaps it would be even better if you would tell me where you won this treasure by your wit."

"That was not the agreement," said he. "Ask me nothing more, for you have received what is due you, as you must truly believe."

10 They laughed and made merry together with praiseworthy courtesy. Soon they went to supper, where there were dainties in plenty. Afterward they sat in the chamber by the hearth, while attendants brought choice wine to them often; and again they agreed jestingly to carry out in the morning the same agreement as before: namely, to exchange their winnings when they met at night, whatever chance befell them or whatever new thing they got. They made the covenant before all the court, while drink
20 to seal the bargain was brought forth with jests. Then they took leave of one another courteously at last, and each man hastened to his bed.

When the cock had crowed and cackled but thrice, the lord leaped from his bed, as did all his attendants. Ere daylight came, as soon as mass and food had been properly despatched, the company repaired to the forest for the chase. The huntsmen's horns were loud as they crossed the plain, and among the thorns they uncoupled the racing hounds.

30 In a copse beside a marsh the hounds soon cried the finding of scent, and the huntsmen with loud shouts encouraged those which first gave tongue. The hounds that heard the noise hastened thither, and fell quickly in pursuit, forty at once. Then rose such a babel and tumult of the hounds in the

pack that the rocks re-echoed. The hunters heart-
ened them with horn and with voice.

In a compact body the hounds rushed forward
between a forest pool and a forbidding crag. On a
rocky hillock beside a cliff, not far from a marshy
thicket, where rough rocks had fallen in confusion,
they found the game at length; and the men came
after them, surrounding both crag and hillock, because they knew well that within the circle was
10 the beast which the bloodhounds had announced.
They beat on the bushes, and bade him rise up,
and he rushed out with disaster to the men in his
path—one of the most marvellous of swine. Long
separated from the herd was the old, old creature,
and savage, the greatest of all boars. When he had
grunted fiercely, he brought trouble to many, for
in his first plunge he knocked three men to the
earth, and sped forth at high speed without pausing.

The hunters called aloud "Hi!" and hallooed
20 "Hay! Hay!", put their horns to their lips, and vigorously blew the assembly call. Many were the merry
voices of men and of hounds, as they rushed noisily
after the boar with threats to kill him. Often he
stood at bay and maimed the pack, injuring the
hounds, while they howled and yelled. Men pressed
forward to shoot at him, loosed their arrows, and
often hit him. But the points failed on his tough
shields, and the barbs would not pierce his brawn,
though the smooth shafts broke in pieces. The ar-
30 row-head rebounded, wherever it hit. Yet when the
blows hurt him, striking so hard, he rushed on the
men in his madness for battle and wounded them in
his rushes, so that many were afraid and withdrew a
little. But the lord on a swift horse dashed after
him, blowing his bugle like the brave man he was
on the hunting-field. He gave the assembly call, and

rode through the thickets, pursuing the wild boar until the sun was high.

Thus through the day they went on, while our gracious knight Gawain lay pleasantly at home in his bed under rich-hued covers. The lady did not forget to come to salute him. Very early she came to cheer his spirits. As she approached the curtain and peeped at the knight, Sir Gawain welcomed her courteously at once. She replied very eagerly, sit-
10 ing down quietly by his side and laughing much.

With a gracious look she said: "Sir, if you are Gawain, it seems wonderful to me that a man so well-disposed at all times to what is good does not understand the manners of society, and that, when instructed by anyone, you put them out of your mind. You have forgotten at once what I taught you yesterday in the best way I could."

"What is that?" quoth the knight. "Truly I do not understand. If what you say be true, I am to
20 blame."

"I instructed you about kissing," said the beautiful lady. "It is proper for any courteous knight to claim a kiss quickly wherever he finds favor."

"My dear lady," quoth the doughty man, "say not so! I dare not do that, lest I be denied. If I were refused, I should surely be wrong in having made the request."

"My faith!" said the merry woman. "You cannot be refused! You are strong enough to get your
30 will by force if you please, should anyone be so ill-bred as to deny you."

"That is all very well, by God," quoth Gawain, "but threats are unlucky in the land where I dwell, and so is any gift not bestowed with good will. I am yours to command, to kiss when you will. You may take kisses when you please, and stop only when it seems to you best."

The lady bowed down and graciously kissed his cheek. Much talk they had of the sorrow and happiness of love.

"If you will not be angry," the noble lady said, "I should like to ask you, sir knight—young and valiant as you are, courteous and chivalrous as you are widely known to be, the best of all knights—
10 why I have never, though I have sat here by you two several times, heard any word from you, less or more, that pertained to love. Yet the chief thing praised in the lore of arms is the faithful sport of love. This labor of true knights is the very title given to their works, and the text of it: how men have ventured their lives for their true love, have endured grievous times of trouble on account of it, and afterward have avenged themselves by their valor and rid themselves of their sorrow, bringing
20 joy into the bower by their virtues. You are known as the most noble knight of your time; your fame and honor are spread abroad everywhere; and you ought, being so gracious and so skilled in courtly vows, to be willing to show and teach a young creature such as I am something about the art of true love. Can it be that you are ignorant, in spite of the fame you bear? Or do you consider me too dull to listen to your courtly conversation? For shame! I have come hither by myself, and here
30 I sit in the hope of learning some craft from you. Teach me, I beg you, out of your wisdom, while my lord is away from home."

"In good faith," quoth Gawain, "may God reward you! My happiness is great, and my pleasure extreme, that so noble a lady should come hither and trouble herself about such a poor man as I am. It

gives me delight that you can amuse yourself with your knight, showing him favor of any kind. But as for taking on myself the task of expounding true love, and preaching about the text and tales of arms, to you who have twice the craft in that art, I know well, than a hundred men such as I am or ever shall be while I live on earth, it would be manifold folly, noble lady, by my troth. As far as I can, I would do what you will, because I am greatly your
10 debtor, and I will be your servant always, so save me the Lord!"

Thus the noble lady made trial of him, and often tempted him to make him woo her, whatever was her intent. But he defended himself so fairly that no fault appeared, nor any wrong on either side, and they were happy together. They laughed and sported for a long time. At last she kissed him, took her leave courteously, and went her way.

Then the knight bestirred himself, and rose for
20 mass, after which their dinner was prepared and splendidly served. The knight amused himself with the ladies all the day; but the lord galloped over the countryside, pursuing his monstrous boar.

The beast rushed along the slopes; and when he stood at bay, snapped asunder the backs of the hounds, till bowmen subdued him and made him plunge on for his life, so many were the arrows shot at him when the hunters collected. Yet at times he made the boldest of them flinch. At last
30 he was so weary that he could run no more, but made as fast as he could for a hollow where a stream ran at the base of a rock. He got the bank at his back and began to paw the earth and whet his white tusks, while the foam frothed horribly at the corners of his mouth. All the brave men disliked to attack from a distance, but they dared not approach

because of his savagery. He had injured so many
before that all were loath to be torn by his tusks.
Fierce he was and mad.

Then came the lord himself, urging on his horse,
and saw the creature at bay, with the group of
men about him. He dismounted with grace, left
his courser, drew out a bright sword, rushed forward, and came fast through the stream where the
enemy had taken his stand. The wild boar saw the
10 man with weapon in hand, and with hair rising he
snorted so violently that many were afraid on the
nobleman's account, lest evil befall him. The pig
rushed, and man and boar were fighting in the
middle of the stream. The boar had the worst of it,
for the man eyed him well when they met, set his
blade straight at the creature's breast, and drove
it up to the hilt, piercing the heart. Snarling he
yielded; and down the stream a hundred hounds
were at him quickly, biting him with fury. The
20 men brought him to the bank, and the dogs gave
tongue to proclaim his death.

The horns blew high triumphal blasts, and the
knights who had breath left hallooed aloud. The
hounds bayed at the creature, as the chief huntsmen of the toilsome chase gave them the signal to
do. Then a man wise in woodcraft began to cut
up the boar with ceremony. First he hewed off
the head and set it aloft, then tore him roughly along
the backbone and took out the guts, which he singed
30 on hot coals. With these, mixed with bread, he
rewarded his hounds. Next he cut out the brawn
in wide slabs, and removed the edible entrails, as
was proper. Then they fastened the halves together
and slung them on a strong pole. Now with their
boar they hastened home. Before the man who

had slain him in the stream by the mighty strength of his hand was borne the head of the beast.

It seemed long to him until he saw Sir Gawain in the hall. He called, and Gawain came towards him to receive his payment. The lord laughed loud and merrily when he saw him, and greeted him joyously. The good ladies were fetched and the household gathered. The lord showed them the slabs of boar's flesh, and told the tale of the wild boar's
10 great size and length, and of his ferocity in the wood where he stood at bay. The other knight commended his deed very courteously and gave him praise for the skill and courage he had shown. Such brawn and such sides, the bold man said, he never before saw taken from any swine. Then they handled the huge head, while the courteous knight admired it and was loud in praise of the lord.

"Now, Gawain," quoth the good man, "this game is yours according to our fixed agreement, as you
20 know well."

"That is so," quoth the knight, "and just as certainly all I have got I shall pass on to you, by my troth." He clasped the nobleman about the neck and graciously kissed him, and a second time did the same. "Now we are fairly quit, this evening," said the knight, "in respect to all the covenants we have solemnly made since I came hither."

The lord said: "By St. Giles, you are the best I know! You will be rich presently, carrying on a
10 trade like this!"

Then they set up tables on trestles and put cloths on them. Bright lights appeared along the walls, where men fastened waxen torches, and the knights were served in the hall. Much noise of merrymaking and joy sprang up about the fire; and both at supper and afterward there were many noble songs such as Christmas processionals and new carols, with all the customary mirth that one can imagine. And ever our courteous knight was beside the lady. She made such an effort to please the stalwart man with her secret looks of favor that he was altogether astonished, and angry inwardly; but on account of his good breeding he could not refuse to be agreeable, but treated her courteously, no matter how twisted the affair became.

10 When they had sported in the hall as long as they pleased, he asked them to his chamber, where they sat by the fire. There they drank, and made game, and the lord proposed the same terms for New Year's Even. The knight craved leave to depart in the morning, for it was near the time when he ought to be gone.

The lord restrained him, bidding him linger, and said: "As I am a true man, I pledge my word, my lord, that you shall reach the Green Chapel, to do 20 your business, long before prime on New Year's Day. So keep to your chamber and take your ease, while I hunt in the forest. I will hold to the terms of our covenant and exchange my gains with you when I return. I have tested you twice, and I find you faithful. Remember, to-morrow morning, that 'The third time pays for all.' Let us make merry and think only of joy while we may, for at any time we may have sorrow."

Gawain promptly agreed to remain, and drink 30 was joyously brought ere they were lighted to their beds. Sir Gawain lay sleeping very softly and quietly through the night; the lord was early dressed, being anxious about his affairs. After mass he and his men took a morsel of food, and in the pleasant morning he called for his mount. All the nobles who were to ride in his train were ready on their

steeds at the gates of the hall. Very lovely was
the earth, for hoar-frost lay on the ground and
the sun rose red from a cloud-bank, while above in
the heavens bright clouds were drifting.

The hunters unleashed the hounds at the edge of
a wood, and the rocks of the forest rang with the
sound of their horns. Some of the hounds fell on
the scent of the fox in cover, but trailed this way
and that to make sure. When a harrier gave tongue,
10 the huntsmen called to him, and his fellows rushed
towards him from all sides, sniffing and running
forward on the right course in a pack. The fox
scuttled before them; but they soon found him,
and when they were in sight went fast away, crying
out on him in their clear, fierce voices. He dodged
and twisted through many a rough wood, doubled
back, and often stopped to listen under the cover
of hedges.

At last he leaped a thorn hedge by a little ditch,
20 stole out very quietly by the edge of a thicket, and
thought by the trick to get away from the hounds
and out of the wood. But then, before he knew it,
he ran upon a hunting station, where three fierce
dogs, all grey, rushed out at him together. He
swerved again quickly, and started fast in a new
direction, going away, much distressed, into the
wood. Then it was joyous sport to listen to the
hounds, when all the pack together were after him.
They set up such a clamor at the sight of him that
30 it seemed all the lofty cliffs had fallen in a heap.
Here he was hallooed, when the knights came up
with him, and was greeted with loud jeers; there
he was threatened and often called a thief; and always the greyhounds were at his tail, not letting
him slacken speed. Often he was chased as he

made for the open, and often he turned suddenly
into cover again, so wily was Reynard.

He led them on like this, indeed, splashed with
mud, the lord and his company, over the mountains
until midday, while the gracious knight at home slept
healthfully through the cold morning within his fair
curtains. But the lady could not sleep for love,
lest the purpose in her heart should fail. She rose
early and came to him in a beautiful mantle splen-
10 didly furred with well-trimmed skins, which reached
to the earth. There were no colored ornaments on
her head, but only the gems that were skilfully
twisted into her fret in clusters of twenty. Her
lovely face and firm throat were bare, as was her
breast both in front and behind. She came into
the chamber and closed the door after her, swung
open a window, and called to the knight with pleasant and cheerful words, rallying him thus: "Ah,
man, how can you sleep when the morning is so
20 clear?"

The noble knight was sunk in gloomy sleep, but
he heard her. He was muttering in the heavy op-
pression of a dream, for he was troubled and distressed with many thoughts of his destiny: how he
was to accomplish his fate the next day at the
Green Chapel, when he should meet the man there
and accept a blow without resistance. But when
the fair lady came, he recovered his wits, came suddenly out his dreams, and quickly answered. The
30 lovely lady approached, laughing sweetly, bent over
his handsome head, and kissed him gracefully. He
welcomed her with courtesy and with excellent cheer,
for she appeared to him so glorious and so gaily
dressed, so faultless in form and so fine in color,
that joy welled up and warmed his heart. With
gentle and courteous smiles they fell into merry

speech, and everything they said was altogether joyous and happy. Much delight they took in the pleasant words that were spoken. If Mary had not been mindful of her knight, there had been great peril for the two. For that noble princess pressed him so continually and was so urgent, that he had either to accept her love or refuse it discourteously. He was concerned about his honor, lest he should be a craven, and yet more about the disaster of
10 committing sin and becoming a traitor to the lord of the castle.

"God guard that may not happen!" quoth the knight. With pleasant laughter he countered all the fond speeches that came from her lips.

Said the lady to the knight: "You deserve blame if you love not the person you lie beside beyond all lovers in the world, unless you have a dearer mistress who pleases you better, and have your faith so plighted to that lady, and set so firmly, that you
20 care not to break the troth—which I nowise believe. I beg that you will now tell me the truth, and by all the loves in the world conceal it not deceitfully."

The knight said, smiling gently: "By St. John, I have no love, in faith, nor will I have one at present."

"That is the worst saying of all," quoth the lady. "But I am answered truly, grievous as it is to me. Graciously kiss me now, and I will go away. All
30 I can do on earth is to mourn, as a woman who greatly loves." Sighing, she bent down and kissed him sweetly, then rose and said as she stood by his side: "Do me this pleasure, my dear, now that I am going away. Give me some gift, your glove perhaps, that I may remember you by it and lessen my grief."

"Now surely," quoth the man, "I would I had here the dearest of my possessions to give you for your love, for you rightly deserve many times over a recompense such as I could not offer. But as to giving you for a love-token what is of such little worth as a glove of Gawain's, it is not honorable for you to have the keepsake at this time; and I am here on a mission in strange lands and have no men with saddle-bags filled with things of worth.
10 That disinclines me to love, my lady, for the present. Each man must do as he is circumstanced. Take it not ill, and do not grieve."

"Nay, gracious and highly honored sir," quoth the lovely lady, "though I have nothing of yours, yet you shall have something of mine."

She offered him a splendid ring made of red gold, set with a brilliant stone that flashed gleams like the bright sun. It was worth, be assured, a very great sum. But the knight refused it, and
20 at once.

"I will accept no gifts now, lovely lady; I have none to offer, and I will take none."

She pressed it on him very earnestly, but he refused her offers, and swore by his honor that he would not have it.

Sorrowful that he would not accept it, she said: "If you refuse my ring because it seems too precious, and you would not be so much beholden to me, I will give you my girdle, which will profit you
30 less."

Quickly she took off a belt that clasped her, bound about her kirtle under the bright mantle. It was fashioned of green silk and ornamented with gold, embroidered only at the edge and adorned with pendants. This she offered to the knight, and besought him merrily to take it, though it was un-

worthy. And he said that he would in no wise
touch either gold or keepsake until God should
send him grace to achieve the adventure he had un-
dertaken.

"Therefore, I pray you, be not displeased, and
do not insist, for I shall never consent to it. I
am greatly beholden to you for your favor, and I
shall be your true servant through heat and cold."

"Are you then refusing this piece of silk," asked
10 the lady, "because it is too simple a thing? So it
seems, to be sure. It is small, and its value is even
less. But anyone who knew the qualities woven
into it would perhaps appraise it at a higher value,
for a man neatly girded with this green belt could
not be slain by any knight under heaven, or by any
means whatsoever."

Then the knight reflected, and it came into his
mind that this would be a treasure on the adventure to which he was destined, when he came to
20 the Green Chapel to receive the return blow. It
would be a noble device if by means of it he could
escape death. So he grew indulgent of her pleading
and let her speak on; and she pressed the belt upon
him and strongly urged him until he consented. She
gave it to him with good will, beseeching him, for
her sake, never to reveal it but to keep it loyally
concealed from her lord. The knight promised
that on no account should anyone ever know aught
of it except the two of them. He thanked her very
30 warmly and earnestly both with heart and mind.
Thereupon she kissed the valiant knight for the third
time, and took her leave, for no more entertainment
was to be got from the man.

When she had gone, Sir Gawain made his prepa-
rations for the day: rose and arrayed himself splendidly, and put away his love-token, the girdle the

lady had given him, hiding it carefully where he
could find it afterward. Then he went straightway
to the chapel, quietly sought out a priest, and begged
to be instructed and taught how his soul might be
saved when he went hence. The priest had from
him a clean confession and showed him his sins,
both the greater and the less, then prayed for mercy
and for his absolution, thereupon absolving him securely and making him as pure of sin as if dooms-
10 day were about to come on the morrow. Then the
knight made more merry among the noble ladies
until nightfall, with seemly carols and every sort of
festivity, than he had done on any day earlier. Every
man had pleasure of him there, and said: "Surely he
was never so joyous since he came hither."

Leave him now in his shelter, where love befell
him! The lord, meanwhile, was pursuing his sport
in the field. He killed the fox that had led him so
long a chase. As he leaped a thorn hedge to get
20 sight of the rascal, following the cry of the hounds
that were hot on the scent, Reynard darted through a
rough grove with the pack racing at his heels. The
lord caught sight of the creature, stopped warily,
and whipping out his bright sword, slashed at the
beast. The animal swerved and would have made
his escape if a hound had not rushed at him before
he could get away. Right before the horse's feet
all the dogs fell on him and worried the crafty beast
with savage din. The lord dismounted briskly and
30 seized the fox, snatching him quickly out of the
mouths of the hounds. He held him high over his
head and gave the halloo, while the pack of furious
dogs bayed at him. Huntsmen with horns came
rushing towards them, blowing the assembly call till
they saw the knight. When the noble company had
come together, all those who had bugles blew at

once, and all the others shouted. It was the merriest baying that man ever heard, the tumult which rose there for Reynard's soul. The hounds had their reward, for they were fondled and their heads were stroked. Then the men took Reynard and stripped off his coat. Thereupon they started homeward, for it was close to nightfall, sounding their mighty horns vigorously.

At length the lord dismounted at his beloved home, and found a fire on the hearth with good Sir Gawain beside it. The knight was happy withal, having enjoyed himself in the friendly company of the ladies. He wore a blue mantle that swept the earth, while his softly furred surcoat became him well; and the hood of the same stuff, which hung on his shoulders, was likewise adorned with fur.

He met the good lord in the centre of the hall, and greeted him merrily, saying with courtesy: "First I will fulfil the agreement that we made as to our good fortune—without sparing drink!" Then he embraced the lord and kissed him three times as coolly and soberly as he could manage.

"By Christ," quoth the other knight, "you have good luck in what you win by this trading, if, that is, you made a good bargain."

"No matter about the price," quoth the other at once. "What I have won I have paid you openly."

"Mary!" quoth the other man. "My winnings are less than yours, for I have hunted all day and have got naught except this foul fox hide. The Devil take it! That is very poor payment for three such treasures as you have pressed heartily upon me here —three such good kisses!"

"Say no more!" quoth Sir Gawain. "I thank you, by the Rood."

As they stood together, the lord told him how the

fox was killed. With mirth and minstrelsy, with good food at their pleasure, they made as merry as men could, with laughter of the ladies and jesting speech, both Gawain and the good lord, so happy were they. As if the company had lost their senses or been drunk, both the lord and his household joked and made merry until the time came when they must separate, for at last they had to go to their beds.

10 Then the noble knight, taking leave of the lord first of all, thanked him courteously. "May the High King reward you for the wonderful sojourn I have had here and for the honor you have done me! If you will please to accept it, I offer myself as your servant. I must needs depart to-morrow, as you know, if you will give me some man according to your promise to show me the road to the Green Chapel, since God wills that I meet my fate there on New Year's Day."

20 "In good faith," quoth the lord, "everything I have ever promised you I will perform with good will."

Thereupon he assigned him a servant to put him on his way and conduct him over the downs, so that he might get through the forest without trouble, and journey by the most direct path. Gawain thanked the lord for the honor he did him, then took his leave of the proud ladies. Sorrowfully he kissed them and made his parting speeches, begging them 30 to accept his hearty thanks. To this they replied in kind, commending him to Christ with grievous sighs. Then he bade farewell ceremoniously to the members of the household, thanking each man in turn for his services and his kindness and the great trouble they had been put to in attendance upon him. And every man was as sorry to part with him as if he had dwelt with him always and been honored by him.

Afterward with attendants and lights he was conducted happily to his chamber and his bed to rest. That he slept soundly I dare not say, for he had much on his mind to reflect upon with reference to the morrow, if he would. Let him lie there. He is close to what he has sought. If you will be patient for a little, I will tell you what happened.

IV

10 Now came the New Year with the passing of night, and day dispersed the darkness, as the Lord willed. But wild weather had risen in the world outside; bitterly the clouds flung their chill on the earth, with enough of the north wind to be a torment to the thinly clad. The snow came shivering down, biting what it touched and nipping the creatures of the wild, while the shrill wind rushed from the heights and filled the valleys with great drifts.

Lying in his bed, the knight listened. Though he 20 shut his eyes, he slept little, but heard the voice of each cock that crew. Ere daybreak he sprang up, for a lighted lamp burned in his chamber. He called for his chamberlain, who answered him promptly, and bade the man fetch him his corslet and saddle his horse. The other quickly brought his weeds and arrayed Sir Gawain carefully. First he put on his clothing to ward off the cold, then his other harness, which had been faithfully kept: the body armor and steel plates polished clean, and 30 the rings of his splendid corslet rolled to free them from rust. All was as fresh as when new; and the knight was fain to give thanks for the care with which each piece had been treated. From here to

Greece no knight was so resplendent when he bade them bring his steed.

Meanwhile he put on the fairest trappings: his coat-armor with its cognizance of bright embroidery worked upon velvet, set and adorned with precious gems, the seams of the coat stitched and the inside lined with beautiful fur. Nor, for his own good, did Gawain forget the girdle, the lady's gift. When he had belted his sword on his sturdy hips, he wound the love-token twice about himself, wrapping the girdle of green silk quickly around his waist. It became the fair knight well, for it showed richly against the fine red cloth. But the man did not put on the belt for display, for pride of the pendants, though they were polished, and though glittering gold shone on the ends of them, but to save himself when he came to the test and had to meet death without being able to defend himself by sword or dagger. Thus prepared, the brave man walked forth from his chamber, thanking all his noble attendants heartily and often.

Gringolet, who had been stabled with care and skill, was ready and eager to be off. The knight went to the proud horse, huge and tall, and examined his coat, then said soberly, swearing it on his honor: "The household in this castle take thought for courtesy. May joy be with the man who keeps them, and love betide the dear lady while she lives! As they have entertained a guest for charity's sake and paid him honor, may the Lord Who rules High Heaven reward them—and also all of you. If I could continue to have life in the world for any time, I should do whatever I could to recompense you."

Then he put his foot into the stirrup and mounted. His attendant passed him his shield, which he slung on his shoulder; and Gringolet, at a touch of

the gilt spurs, no longer stood prancing but leaped forward on the pavement. Bearing his spear and lance, the knight on his steed commended the castle to Christ and asked good fortune for it. The drawbridge was let down, and both sides of the wide gates were unbarred and flung open. When he had made the sign of the cross, the knight rode out over the planks of the bridge, thanking the porter, who knelt and bade him good-bye, commending him to
10 Christ for safety.

Thus the prince went on his way accompanied only by the man who was to guide him to the dismal place where he must receive the grievous blow. They passed along the hillslopes beneath the bare boughs of the trees; they mounted by cliffs in the penetrating cold. The clouds hung high, but the weather beneath them was threatening. On the moors there were damp mists, and on the mountains fell drizzling rain. Each hill was capped with a huge
20 cloak of fog. The brooks boiled and foamed against their banks, dashing and breaking as they plunged downward. Very perplexing was the way the men followed through the forest until sunrise, which found them on a high hill with an expanse of white snow before them. The attendant bade his master halt.

"I have brought you hither, sir knight, and now you are not far from the famous place for which you have inquired and sought with so much zeal.
30 Since I know you and you are a lord whom I love well, I will tell you truly that you would do better to follow my advice. The place you are hastening to is thought extremely perilous. The worst man in the world dwells in that wild spot. He is strong and grim and loves to give a blow, he is taller than any other man in the world—more huge of body

than any four in Arthur's house, Hector, or any
other. He so manages at the Green Chapel that
no man, however proud, can ride by the place without being slain by a blow from his hand, for he is
ruthless and has no mercy. Be he churl or chaplain
who passes by, monk or priest, or any other man, he
likes as well to kill him as to live himself. As truly
as you are sitting in your saddle, I tell you, you shall
be killed when you come there if he can accomplish
10 it, though you had twenty lives to spend. Trust
what I say. He has lived here long and done much
harm by his fighting. Against his terrible blows
you cannot defend yourself. Therefore, good Sir
Gawain, let the man alone, and for God's sake go
away by some other road and seek some other land.
May Christ speed you! I will hasten home again,
and I promise you further—and I will swear it
by God and all his good saints, so help me God
and the holy relics and plenty of other oaths!—
20 that I will keep your counsel loyally and never
set going any tale about how you fled from any man,
as far as I know."

"Many thanks," quoth Gawain, and he spoke re-
provingly. "May good befall you, my man, for
wishing me well, and I believe you would loyally
keep my counsel. But if you kept it ever so secret,
and I fled away for fear while passing here as you
suggest, I should be a coward knight and not to be
excused. Whatever may befall, I will go to the
30 Chapel and hold with the man the conversation that
I please, be it for weal or woe as fate may decree.
Although he be a grim fellow to deal with, and
stand there with a club, the Lord may full well
save his servants."

"Mary!" quoth the other man. "Since you say at
such length that you will take your own hurt on

yourself, and if you wish to lose your life, I will not hinder or hold you back. Put your helmet on your head and take your spear in your hand, and ride down this same path by the side of yonder cliff until you come to the bottom of the wild valley. Then look a little across the glade on the left side, and you shall see the Chapel itself in the valley and the sturdy man who keeps it. Now farewell, noble Gawain, with God's blessing! I would not go with
10 you for all the gold on earth, nor bear you fellowship through this wood a foot further."

With that, the man turned his horse in the forest, hit him with his heels as hard as ever he could, and galloped away, leaving the knight there by himself.

"By God Himself," quoth Gawain, "I will neither cry out nor lament. I bow myself to God's will and commit myself to Him."

Then he spurred Gringolet and followed down
20 the path, making his way by a bank on the edge of the wood and riding forward along the rough slope straight into the dale. There he paused to look about, for the place seemed deserted; and he saw no sign of habitation, but only steep and high banks on both sides and rough crags knobbed with jutting rocks. The clouds seemed to him to graze the crags. Reining in his horse, he halted and looked this way and that, in search of the Chapel. He saw nothing of the kind on any side, which seemed to
30 him strange; but soon he descried, a little way down a glade, something like a mound, a broad hillock on the bank of a stream, near a waterfall that tumbled down there. The brook bubbled as if it were boiling.

The knight urged on his steed and came to the mound, where he dismounted and tied the rein of his horse to a rough branch. Then he went to the mound and walked about it, debating within himself what it might be. It had a hole in one end and holes on each side, and was overgrown everywhere with patches of grass. Inside, it was hollow—nothing but an old cave or a crevice in a crag, he could not determine which.

"Lord!" quoth the gentle knight. "Whether or not this be the Green Chapel, the Devil might well say his matins here at midnight! Surely this is a 10 desolate place, an ugly oratory overgrown with weeds. It well befits the man in green to make his devotions here after the devil's use. Now I feel sure by all my five senses that it is the Fiend who has trapped me into this covenant in order to destroy me. This is a chapel of misfortune, ill luck take it! It is the cursedest church that ever I came to."

With his tall helmet on his head and with lance in hand, he went up to the rough rocks of the place. Then he heard from a crag on the slope of a high 20 hill beyond the brook a marvellously loud noise. Lo! it clattered as if it would split the cliff apart, like someone sharpening a scythe on a grindstone. Lo! it whirred and made a grinding noise, like water at a mill. Lo! it rang and rushed at the same time— something terrible to hear.

"By God," quoth Gawain, "that contrivance, I think, is being made ready for our meeting, sir knight, according to our agreement. Let God bring weal or woe, it helps me in no wise to be afraid. 30 Though I lose my life, no noise shall frighten me."

Then the knight called out very loud: "Who has a mind to hold tryst with me in this place? Good Gawain is walking here. If any man wishes aught of him, let him hasten hither to do his business, either now or never."

"Stay," quoth someone on the bank above his

head, "and you shall quickly receive all that I once promised."

Yet he went on with the rushing noise for a short time, and changed to the sound of whetting before he would come down. At length he made his way along a crag and came out of one of the holes, brandishing as he emerged a terrible weapon—a newly sharpened Danish axe—wherewith to give the blow. It had a heavy bit, four feet wide, curved back in line with the helve and sharpened with a whetstone. It was no smaller than the one used before, if measured by the gleaming thong; and the man in green was arrayed in the same way, both face and legs, hair and beard, except that he advanced on foot, setting the handle of the axe on the stones and marching beside it. When he came to the stream, he would not wade across, but vaulted over by the help of his axe, and came forward rapidly over the snow-covered ground in a fury. Gawain met the knight, but did not bow to him.

The green man said: "Now, sweet sir, one may trust you to keep an agreement. God must guard you, Gawain! You are truly welcome to my place, and you have timed your journey as a loyal man should. You know the covenant between us. A twelvemonth ago you took what came to you, and at this New Year I was to be promptly repaid. We are here in this valley altogether by ourselves. There are no men at hand to separate us, no matter what we do. Take off your helmet and receive your payment, nor make more resistance than I offered when you struck off my head at one blow."

"Nay," quoth Gawain, "by God Who gave me life, I shall in no way bear ill will for any hurt that comes. If you confine yourself to one blow. I shall stand still and make no resistance to your doing what you please."

He bent forward, bowing, and showed the flesh of his neck all bare, pretending not to be afraid. He would not flinch for terror. Then the man in green made ready quickly, lifting up his grim weapon to smite Gawain. With all the strength in his body he raised it aloft, making a mighty feint of destroying him. Had it fallen as powerfully as he pre-
10 tended to make it, the ever valiant knight would have been slain by the blow. But Gawain glanced sidelong at the axe as it came rushing down through the air to destroy him, and flinched a little from the sharp steel with his shoulders. The other man, with a sudden jerk, pulled back the bright blade, and reproved the prince with many scornful words.

Quoth he: "You are not Gawain, who is held so good a knight and never quailed at any force on hill or in valley, for now you flinch with terror before
20 you feel any hurt. I have never heard such cowardice reported of that knight. I did not flinch or draw back, man, when you took aim, nor did I raise any difficulty in King Arthur's house. My head dropped to my feet, and yet I never flinched. Yet you, before you have received any harm, are terrified in heart. Wherefore I am to be reckoned the better man."

Quoth Gawain: "I flinched once, but I will do so no more. Only I cannot restore my head if it falls
30 to the ground. But make haste, man, in faith, and come to the point with me. Give me my destiny, and do it out of hand, for I shall wait your stroke and not move again till your axe has hit me. You have my pledge."

"Have at you, then!" quoth the other, and raised the axe aloft, looking as furious as if he were mad.

He feinted at his man mightily, but did not cleave him, withholding his hand just before the stroke fell. Gawain waited it steadfastly and did not flinch at all, but stood like a stone, or like a stump which is fastened in rocky ground by a hundred roots.

Then the man in green said playfully: "Since your heart is so steadfast, it behooves me to strike. Hold fast to the noble knighthood that Arthur gave you, and keep your neck at this blow if you can
10 manage it."

Fiercely angry, Gawain replied: "Smite on, you cruel man! You threaten too long. I believe that your own heart is terrified."

"Truly," quoth the other man, "you speak so fiercely that I will no longer delay your business."

Then he took his stance to give the blow, with a frown on lip and forehead. No wonder that Gawain, hoping for no rescue, was troubled. The green man raised his weapon lightly and let the cutting
20 edge of the blade drop squarely on the bare neck. Though the stroke was fierce, it did no more hurt than to give him a scratch, for the blade merely cut through the skin and the outer layer of flesh. And when he saw the bright blood spurting over his shoulders and gleaming on the snow, he sprang forward more than a spear-length in a sudden leap, clutched his helmet quickly and placed it on his head, slipped his shield into place on his shoulder, pulled out his bright sword, and fiercely spoke. Never in the world
30 since he had been born of his mother had he been half so happy a man.

"Cease, man, to strike! Threaten me no more! I have taken one blow here without resistance, and if you give me another, I shall promptly return it, requiting you without hesitation—fiercely, too, you may be sure. One stroke only I owe you, as the covenant made in Arthur's hall provided. Stop, then, good sir!"

The knight moved away and rested on his axe, setting the helve on the ground and leaning on the blade. He looked at the prince, who was ready for battle, saw how boldly he stood there armed, doughty, fearless, and completely without dread. In his heart he was pleased.

Then in a loud, ringing tone he said playfully to the knight: "Bold man, be not so fierce. No one here has ill-used you or treated you discourteously, except as the covenant of the king's court provided. I promised you a stroke, and you have it. Consider yourself well requited. I release you from the remainder of all other rights. If I had not been skilful, I might perhaps have given you a worse blow and done you harm. In the first place I threatened you merely and did not cleave you with a sore wound (which I might have given you rightfully) because of the agreement we made on our first night together, and because you kept faith with me loyally and justly, passing on to me all your gains as a good man should. The second threat I offered you, man, because of the morning when you kissed my beautiful wife—the kisses came back to me! For both of them I gave you mere feints without doing you harm. An honest man gives back honestly, and need fear no danger. The third time you failed, and for that you should accept the tap I gave you.

"The woven girdle you wear is mine. My own wife gave it to you, as I know well. I know well, too, your kisses, and all your behavior, and my wife's wooing of you. I arranged it myself. I sent her to test you, and methinks you are truly one of the most flawless men who ever stepped on foot. As a pearl is of more value than a white pea, so is Gawain,

in truth, when compared with other fair knights.
Here you failed a little, sir, and were wanting in
loyalty! but that was on account of no intrigue, or
love-making either, but because you loved your life.
I blame you the less."

The other brave man stood in meditation for a
great while, so grieved and mortified that his heart
cried out in anguish within him. All the blood of
his breast streamed into his face, and he winced for
10 shame while the knight spoke.

The first words he uttered were these: "Cursed
be cowardice and covetousness both! Lack of chivalry and the vice that destroys knightly virtue are
in them." Then he took hold of the knot of the
belt, loosened the fastening, and thrust it violently
at the man. "Lo! there is the faith-breaker! Evil
befall it! For fear of your blow, cowardice taught
me to make a pact with covetousness, forsaking my
proper nature—the generosity and loyalty which be-
20 fit knights. Now am I guilty and disloyal, I who
have ever been afraid of nothing save treachery and
lack of truth. Sorrow and care come to both! I
acknowledge to you, sir knight, here between us
two, that my behavior has been altogether faulty.
If you will restore me to your good will, I will be
more wary hereafter."

Then the other lord laughed and said courteously:
"I consider the wrong I received completely
amended. You have made a clean confession, ac-
30 knowledging your mistakes, and have done your penance at the point of my sword. I regard you as
cleansed of your offence, as well purified as if you
had never done wrong since you were first born. I
give you the gold-bordered belt, sir, for it is green
like my robe. You may recall this contest, Sir
Gawain, as you journey among famous princes; and

for chivalrous knights this girdle will serve as a token of the adventure of the Green Chapel. You must come again to my house this New Year. We shall revel very pleasantly during the remainder of the noble festival." The lord urged him to come, saying: "I think we can make your peace with my wife, who was your bitter foe!"

"Nay, forsooth," quoth the knight, seizing his helmet and courteously removing it, while he thanked the nobleman. "I have stayed long enough. Happiness be yours! May He Who is the author of all honor reward you! Commend me to that gracious lady, your lovely wife, both to her and to the other, my honored ladies, who have so adroitly beguiled their knight by their trick. It is no wonder though a fool behave with folly and be brought to grief by the wiles of women, for so was Adam deceived by one during his life and Solomon by many, and Samson in turn was brought to his doom by Delilah, and David afterwards was deluded by Bathsheba and suffered much sorrow. Now these men were brought to disaster by the wiles of women. It were altogether best, if a man could, to love them well and believe them not. For these men were the noblest of old, and all of them followed wisdom beyond all other men under heaven who have given themselves to thought; yet were they all deceived by the women they knew. Though I have been deluded, it seems to me I may be excused.

"But your girdle! God give you thanks! I will keep it with good will, not for the beautiful gold, or the barrings, or the silk, or the long pendants, for neither the richness nor the honor nor the lovely ornament; but in token of my wrong-doing I shall look at it often when I ride forth in splendor, thus recalling to my mind the frailty and faultiness of the perverse flesh, how liable it is to the stain of impurity. Thus, when pride shall stir me on account of prowess in arms, looking on this love-token will humble my heart. But one thing I would pray you, if you will not be displeased by my asking. Since you are lord of yonder region where I have been honorably entertained by you—may the Lord, Who upholds heaven and sits on high, reward you for it!—what is your right name? I ask no more."

10 "I will tell you truly," quoth the other then. "I am called Bercilak de Hautdesert in this land. Morgan la Fay, who dwells in my house, has acquired many of the arts of Merlin through the power and skill of her learning, and has learned his magic well, for she has had pleasant passages of love of old with that excellent clerk, who knows all your knights at home. Therefore she is called Morgan the Goddess. No one has such lofty pride that she cannot tame him. She sent me in this guise to your delight-
20 ful hall, in order to test the pride and the truth of the great renown of the Round Table. She arranged this marvel to take away your wits; to grieve Guenevere and cause her to die with terror of that man—the phantom who spoke with his head in his hand before the high table. She is the ancient dame at home, and she is your aunt, too, Arthur's half-sister, the daughter of the Duchess of Tintagel, by whom noble Uther afterward had the now glorious Arthur. Therefore I beg you, sir knight, to
30 come to your aunt and make merry in my house. The people in my court love you, and for your great fidelity I love you as well as any man under God, by my honor."

But Gawain refused him. He would in no wise do it. They embraced, and kissed, and commended each other to the Prince of Paradise, and parted straightway with regret. Gawain on his fair steed rode boldly towards the castle of the king, and the knight all in green whithersoever he would.

Now Gawain, having won the grace of his life, rode Gringolet by wild ways through the world. Often he lodged indoors and often outside, had many adventures by the way, and gained so many victories that I do not intend to recount them now. The hurt he had received in his neck was made whole; and he 10 wore the gleaming belt bound slantwise like a baldric by his side and tied with a knot under his left arm, in token of the spot of wrong-doing by which he had been overcome.

Thus in sound health the knight reached the court. Joy awoke in the house when the great king heard that Gawain had come. He was glad and kissed the knight, as did the queen also, and afterward many brave knights came to embrace him and ask him about his fortune. He told the marvels of it, re-20 counting all the hardships he had experienced, the adventure of the Chapel, the behavior of the knight, the lady's love-making, and at last the story of the girdle. Although he suffered agony when he had to tell of it, and groaned with sorrow and mortification, he bared his neck to show the little cut he had received at the lord's hands as a rebuke for his disloyalty. His face flushed with shame as he showed the mark.

"Lo, my lord," quoth the knight, and touched 30 the girdle, "this is the symbol of the fault for which my neck is scarred, of the hurt and damage I have received, of the cowardice and covetousness with which I was there overcome. This is the token of the disloyalty in which I was caught. I must needs wear it while I live, for none may conceal his wrong-doing without harm coming of it, since where wrong-doing has fastened itself it will never depart."

The king comforted the knight, and all the court laughed loud at the tale. Then the lords and ladies of the Table courteously agreed that each man of the brotherhood should wear a band of bright green slantwise about him like a baldric, and this on account of that knight and in imitation of him. The Round Table gave the baldric renown, and ever after he who wore it was honored, as is told in the
10 best books of romance. Thus in Arthur's day this adventure took place, and the Bruts bear witness to it. Since the bold warrior Brutus first came hither, after the siege and assault of Troy had come to an end, many such adventures have occurred. Now He Who wore the crown of thorns bring us to joy with Him! Amen.

HONI SOYT QUI MAL PENCE

NOTES

NOTES

The following notes are intended as a supplement to those interspersed with the text, not as a substitute for them. Although the editor trusts that they may not be found necessary to an intelligent reading of the selections, he hopes that they will be useful. In so far as they are explanatory, they deal for the most part with matters of literary construction and the like, which could not well be discussed in foot-notes. The opportunity has also been taken to supply brief suggestive bibliographies.

OLD ENGLISH LITERATURE

The student who knows no Old English but who wishes to learn more about pre-Conquest literature may read with profit the admirable translations in J. D. Spaeth's *Old English Poetry* (Princeton Univ. Press), 1921, where he will find also much illuminating comment. For the prose, Cook and Tinker, *Select Translations from Old English Prose* (Ginn), 1908, may be commended. The best general survey of the literature remains that of B. ten Brink, *Early English Literature*, translated by H. M. Kennedy. Stopford Brooke, *History of Early English Literature*, 1892, and *English Literature from the Beginning to the Norman Conquest*, 1898, may be read for his stimulating aesthetic criticism, though his knowledge and judgment are often at fault. Excellent books dealing with the Middle English period as well are W. P. Ker, *English Literature: Mediaeval* (Home University Library), C. S. Baldwin, *Three Medieval Centuries of Literature in England*, 1932, and W. W. Lawrence, *Medieval Story*, 2nd ed. 1926. For the history of the period, see C. Oman, *England before the Norman Conquest*, 1913. For the life of the Germanic tribes, see F. B. Gummere, *Founders of England*, rev. ed., 1930.

BEOWULF

The best editions of the original text are those by Wyatt and Chambers, 1920, and F. Klaeber, 1928, which contain much valuable illustrative material. Indispensable to an adequate knowledge of the poem is W. W. Lawrence, *Beowulf and the Epic Tradition,* 1928. To be recommended also are R. W. Chambers, *Beowulf, an Introduction,* 2nd ed., 1932, and H. M. Chadwick, *The Heroic Age,* 1912. For the relations between heroic poetry and later narrative verse, see W. P. Ker, *Epic and Romance,* 1897, and W. M. Dixon, *English Epic and Heroic Poetry,* 1912.

The main story that lies behind the poem of *Beowulf* was perhaps brought to northern England by belated colonists in the sixth century. At all events, real events that took place in that century are imbedded in it, and they are wholly Continental. Of this much we can be reasonably sure: somewhere in the northern lands tradition wove about the person of a purely fictitious Beowulf a web of high adventure. He was made a great king of the Geats, somewhat as Arthur in later centuries was made a great king of the Britons; he was endowed with supernatural powers and made the ideal hero of his race. Probably some of his exploits had earlier been told of a vaguely remembered demi-god called Beowa, whom the Angles would have known before their migration across the North Sea. The story, somewhat as we have it, must certainly have been known in England for a considerable time before the author of *Beowulf* took it in hand. The names show this, as do certain changes wrought in the legends themselves, which can be checked by reference to Continental versions of the tales. Whether the English poet had lays to work with, or only oral tradition, we have no means whatever of knowing. All we can say is that he made from heroic material of diverse origin an epic in which the point of view is that of christianized Anglia at the end of the seventh century. He was a Christian, but he had not forgotten the traditions of an older day. His pictures of court life, as well as of adventure, idealize the life of the past times but are based on knowledge of his own.

Pp. 10-11, vv. 1-85. This introductory passage gives the genealogy of the kings of the Danes, or Scyldings, whose glory has to be emphasized in order to show the significance of the hero's exploits in rescuing Hrothgar from calamity. It will be noted that the Danish king Beowulf has no connection with the hero of the poem. The Danes occupied in the sixth century an ill-defined region, of which the island of Zealand in Denmark was the centre. This was the country from which the Angles had migrated earlier. Of all the tribes left on the Continent, the Danes seem to have been the closest to the inhabitants of northern England. There is reason to believe that Hrothgar was a real king, though his magnificence is of course purely imaginary.

P. 13, v. 78. Hart, or Heorot, probably because adorned with stags' antlers on the gables.

V. 102. Grendel, half man and half beast, is a strange combination of pagan superstitions and Old Testament lore.

Pp. 15-16, vv. 175-188. Quite inconsistently, the author here represents the Danes as pagans, though elsewhere they are shown to be Christians.

P. 16, vv. 194-19. Hygelac's kinsman Beowulf was the son of Ecgtheow, a Wægmunding, who had married a princess of the Geats or Wethers. The Geats probably lived in what is now Sweden. Hygelac was certainly an historic king, who made an unsuccessful raid against the Franks about 516. He was succeeded by his son Heardred, after whom Beowulf came to the throne.

Pp. 17-25, vv. 229-498. The stately dignity of Beowulf's reception should be noted. Something like these would have been the manners at a Northumbrian court in the poet's time. It is doubtful whether they would have been so good in sixth-century Denmark. Throughout the poem, indeed, the manners pictured are less primitive than the events of the story would lead us to expect.

P. 21, vv. 373-375. This method of explaining relationships is quite characteristic. Not until this point do we learn that Beowulf was a Geat on the maternal side, and only later do we find that his father was a Wægmunding.

P. 23, vv. 433-439. This is the first reference to the hero's superhuman strength of hand, which is mentioned in connection with all his adventures. See 2682-2687.

P. 24, v. 454. Weland was the Germanic Vulcan. Nothing better could be said of armor or weapons than that they were the work of Weland. His fame lived on in popular legend, which accounts for the name of the cromlech in the Vale of the White Horse in Berkshire, Wayland Smith's Forge.

Vv. 459-472. This reference to Ecgtheow's feud is brought in to emphasize the traditional friendship between Geats and Danes.

Pp. 25-28, vv. 499-605. Unferth's unmannerly and inaccurate taunt gives Beowulf an opportunity to tell the true story of his swimming contest with Breca and of his encounter with sea-monsters, which prepares us for his struggle with Grendel. Unferth is not represented consistently. See 1165-1168, 1455-1472, 1807-1812.

P. 30, vv. 677-685. A conventional boasting speech in the heroic tradition. See 1392-1396 and 2510-2537.

Pp. 31-35, vv. 703-836. The fight with Grendel, the climax of the first adventure.

P. 35, vv. 841-852. Compare this description of the pool of the monsters with the later impressions at 1345-1382, 1416-1440, 1591-1625.

P. 36, v. 870. Note the reference to alliterative verse, like that in which *Beowulf* is written.

Pp. 36-37, vv. 874-915. After the celebration in song of Beowulf's own exploit, there follows the summary of a lay made about Sigemund. The report of it here implies that Beowulf ranked among the greatest of Germanic heroes. The lay related Sigemund's adventures in general, especially those in which he was accompanied by his nephew Fitela (his son, according to the later Norse *Volsungasaga*), and secondly his famous dragon-fight. This dragon-fight recalls the one attributed to his son Sigurth or Siegfried, which has become better known in modern times. The story ends by saying that Sigemund's fame succeeded that of the Danish king Heremod, about whom more is later told by Hrothgar (See 1709-1722). Heremod appears as a king of brilliant promise, who became mean and cruel before he met his end.

P. 38, vv. 942-946. See Luke xi, 27.

Pp. 38-39, vv. 957-979. This speech of Beowulf's, rehearsing what has already been narrated, is in keeping with the spacious manner of epics. Beowulf tells the same story again at 2069-2100. Similar repetitions may be found in the *Odyssey*.

P. 40, v. 1017. Hrothulf was the nephew of Hrothgar and succeeded him on the throne.

Pp. 41-44, vv. 1065-1159. This passage reports in somewhat elliptical fashion the second of the lays sung at the feast in Heorot. A band of Danes under Hnæf, while guests of Finn, the king of the Frisians (Eotens or Jutes), were attacked by night, and Hnæf was slain, together with a son of Finn. His followers remained at the Frisian court through the winter, having made a truce with Finn. In the spring the Danes became restless and under the leadership of Hengest fell on the Frisians, killing Finn and carrying away to

Denmark Queen Hildeburh, who was Finn's wife and Hnæf's sister. Apparently this second fight was precipitated by the coming of Guthlaf and Oslaf, perhaps with Danish reinforcements. Another and slightly different account of the first battle may be found in the fragmentary *Fight at Finnsburh*.

P. 44, vv. 1163-1168. These lines have three stresses instead of two in each half-verse, as do 1705-1707 and 2995-2996 in the original text.

Pp. 45-46, vv. 1197-1214. The necklace that Wealhtheow gave to Beowulf is compared with one carried off by Hama from Eormenric, a famous king of the East Goths. By anticipation the poet tells what became of it after it was presented by Beowulf to Hygd, the wife of Hygelac. See 2172-2173.

P. 50, vv. 1345-1376. Hrothgar's account of Grendel's mere is one of the best examples in Old English poetry of what may be called impressionistic description. In such passages, which are of frequent occurrence, clearness of visualization is sacrificed to emotional appeal, very much as it is in some modern romantic poetry. The same method, applied to passages of action, accounts for what we may term the stuttering effect of much narrative verse in Old English. But what is lost in clarity is gained in vividness and intensity of feeling.

Pp. 57-58, vv. 1615-1617. Notice that it is the blood of Grendel rather than that of his less powerful mother, by which the sword is melted.

P. 60, vv. 1687-1698. The mysterious sword found in the sea-cavern was properly engraved with the record of men before the Flood, since it belonged to Grendel, who was a descendant of Cain.

Pp. 60-62, vv. 1700-1784. This speech of Hrothgar's, which praises Beowulf by contrasting him with Heremod, who had already been used as a monitory example by the minstrel after Grendel's death, has been criticized as being out of key with the mood of rejoicing at the court. This is to neglect the solemnity with which the second episode of the poem concludes. Hrothgar warns Beowulf, to be sure, but chiefly of the transitory nature of worldly prosperity, citing what he himself has endured in life. Thus considered, the passage is highly dramatic. Note that the departure of Beowulf, which follows, is given a similar tone of high seriousness.

Pp. 67-68, vv. 1926-1962. Hygelac's wife, Queen Hygd, the daughter of Hæreth, is here introduced by contrasting her with Thryth, who after a violent youth became the well-conducted wife of Offa. The story of Thryth is obscure in its details, but of special interest in that Offa was an Anglian king. This passage is thus the only one in the poem that treats any distinctively English tradition.

Pp. 69-71, vv. 2020-2069. The first passage of prophecy in the poem. Beowulf, in mentioning Hrothgar's daughter Freawaru, who was not described in the scenes at the Danish court, was led to speak of her betrothal to a prince of the Heathobards (Battle-Bards), the son of Froda, in order to heal a feud. He forecasts that some old warrior will taunt the Heathobards when he sees a Danish follower of the princess with a sword taken in the old wars, and that fighting will again break out.

Pp. 71-72, vv. 2069-2094. This third account of the victory over Grendel adds the detail of the sack carried by the monster, as well as the name of his victim Handscio.

P. 74, v. 2179. The reference is to King Heremod, already twice mentioned by the poet.

Vv. 2183-2189. This statement as to Beowulf's youth corresponds to nothing else told about him, though such backwardness is a commonplace in the biographies of heroes. See the stories about Offa and the early stages of the Hamlet legend.

P. 75, v. 2200. The third episode of the poem begins at this point.

Pp. 75-78, vv. 2212-2311. The history of the dragon-hoard is learned from this passage and from 3047-3073. The two accounts do not agree about the original possessor of the treasure. According to the later passage "famous princes" placed the gold in the barrow, whereas according to the earlier one the last survivor of a tribe buried it there. Attempts to reconcile the two versions are futile. At all events, the treasure lay in the earth for a thousand years, guarded for the last three hundred by the dragon. Then a fugitive from justice found it by chance and brought an ornamented beaker to his lord as a peace-offering. This theft angered the dragon and led to his devastation of Beowulf's kingdom. The barrow is described as built on a height, a structure of stone covered by a mound of earth. Inside was a chamber of some size (see 2717-2719) containing the treasure. The whole is called "the work of giants," a term by which our ancestors designated not only such remains of the Stone Age as this, but also the decayed ruins of Roman work, which must have been common enough in the eighth century.

Pp. 79-80, vv. 2354-2367. The death of Hygelac on his

expedition against the Frisians, referred to at 1205-1214, is again mentioned at 2502-2508 and 2914-2921. Beowulf's feat appears only here.

P. 80, vv. 2379-2396. These wars with the Swedes are described also at 2202-2206, 2472-2489, 2611-2625, and 2922-2998. They may be sketched as follows: In the time of Hæthcyn, Hrethel's son, the Swedes under Ongentheow attacked the Geats. The Geats made reprisals, and Hæthcyn was killed. Hygelac, his brother, then came up and rescued the Geat forces in Ravenswood, where they had taken refuge. In this skirmish Ongentheow was killed by the brothers Eofor and Wulf. After Hygelac's death, Heardred received Eanmund and Eadgils, sons of Ohtere, who had fled from their uncle Onela, the second son of Ongentheow. Onela invaded Geatland and killed both Heardred and Eanmund, letting Beowulf assume the royal power. Later Eadgils, assisted by the Geats, attacked Onela, killed him, and took over the Swedish throne.

P. 89, v. 2679. Names for swords are common in heroic legend. Unferth gave Beowulf the sword called Hrunting (see 1455-1464 and 1807-1812). Similarly Balmung is the name of Sigurd's sword in the *Nibelungenlied*, and Miming of Siegfried's in the *Thidrekssaga*. Nor is Beowulf's unfortunate tendency to have swords fail him at need (see 1522) altogether unexampled. Similar overpowering strength was attributed to Sigurd and Offa.

P. 92, vv. 2802-2808. Such funeral mounds are mentioned in the *Iliad* and the *Odyssey*.

Pp. 93-95, vv. 2845-2891. The cowards had broken the basic law of the Germanic peoples in thus deserting their leader. Wiglaf's reproaches are not too severe.

CYNEWULF

For an account of Old English poetry on Christian themes, see A. J. Barnouw, *Anglo-Saxon Christian Poetry,* translated by Louise Dudley, 1914.

AN ADVENT HYMN

Pp. 104-105. This passage is from Christ, vv. 378-415. The best edition of the poem is that by A. S. Cook, 1900. For a prose translation of all the Cynewulfian poetry, see C. W. Kennedy, *The Poems of Cynewulf,* 1910, which also contains a valuable introduction.

CONSTANTINE'S VISION

Pp. 105-110. This passage from *Elene* occurs at the beginning of the poem and includes vv. 1-147. The best edition is that of A. S. Cook, *The Old English Elene, Phœnix, and Physiologus,* 1919. For some account of the adaptation of such material in Old English, see the editor's *Saints' Legends,* 1916, pp. 55-93. The poem proceeds with the story of the adventures of Queen Helena, who goes to Jerusalem at her son's command to recover the true cross.

THE WANDERER

Pp. 110-113. The translation of this noble poem is from J. D. Spaeth, *Old English Poetry,* 1921, pp. 140-144. The text may be found in any Old English reader.

MIDDLE ENGLISH LITERATURE

See W. H. Schofield, *English Literature from the Norman Conquest to Chaucer,* 1906, as well as the following, which have a wider scope: W. P. Ker, *English Literature: Mediaeval* (Home University Library), C. S. Baldwin, *Three Medieval Centuries of Literature in England,* 1932, W. W. Lawrence, *Medieval Story,* 2nd ed. 1926.

THE VISION OF PIERS PLOWMAN

Pp. 114-125. The edition of W. W. Skeat in two volumes (1886) contains all three versions of the poem.

P. 115, l. 5. A. H. Bright, in *New Light on Piers Plow-man,* 1928, argues plausibly for the identification of a certain valley in the Malvern Hills as the one the author had in mind.

P. 116, l. 10. *Qui loquitur turpiloquium,* he who utters obscenity, which is not a quotation from St. Paul, as a careless reading of the text might make one think.

L. 15. *knaves of Robert,* a common term for thievish vagabonds in the fourteenth century.

L. 26. *the friars.* See Chaucer's sketch, pp. 208-210.

P. 117, l. 5. *a pardoner.* See Chaucer's Pardoner, pp. 223-225, 249-268.

L. 21. *time of the pestilence,* probably the Black Death of 1348-9.

P. 118, l. 16. *Dieu vous save,* the refrain of a popular song, significantly in French.

THE PEARL

Pp. 127-132. There are editions of the poem by C. G. Osgood, 1906, and Sir I. Gollanz, revised 1921. Translations by Gollanz in the edition named, and by G. G. Coulton, 1906.

SIR GAWAIN AND THE GREEN KNIGHT

Pp. 132-199. The poem is now available in an excellent edition by J. R. R. Tolkien and E. V. Gordon, 1930. The reader should observe how carefully the author has arranged his material. The division of the romance into four parts is not arbitrary, for each part represents a different stage of the narrative and contributes to the organic symmetry of the whole. Even the hunting scenes in the third part, with detail so exact that it would have satisfied any fourteenth-century hunting knight, though they seem a little overwrought to us, are justified by the way they balance the encounters between Gawain and Bercilak's wife. Chaucer himself never wrote a narrative more structurally perfect. Similarly, the conversations throughout the poem are admirable not only in the way they preserve the accent of real speech but advance the action. Although the plot is fantastic, the ways of the people involved are the ways of medieval lords and ladies, not the movements of puppets. A vein of humor, one should not fail to notice, runs throughout the story, appearing both in conversation and in event. The author had the happy gift of treating serious issues and ideals without pulling a long face. He made excellent use, too, of the possibilities of verse by way of heightening and intensifying his story. The reader of any prose translation must take this important element on trust, but he should not forget it.

Pp. 132-133. The opening stanzas were probably not too seriously intended. To place Arthur in the succession of British kings was the conventional thing to do. "This," the author says in effect, "is to be a tale from the dignified history of our island." He then pictures immediately a very gay young Arthur surrounded by light-hearted courtiers. Notice that he returns to the *Brut* at the end of the poem (p. 199).

Pp. 136-138. One accepts the supernatural here, as throughout the tale, because it is so naturally introduced against a background of reality. The circumstantial detail, moreover, lulls us into credulity.

Pp. 147-152. The arming of Gawain is a careful account of the ritual proper to such occasions. It should be noted that the knight was equipped according to the latest fashion of the fourteenth century. The elaborate comment on the pentangle and its significance serves the same end: to dignify Gawain and emphasize the seriousness of his quest. The effect of this is heightened by the description of his journey, which follows. In the original this latter passage is romantic poetry of a high order.

Pp. 152-161. The description of the castle, as Gawain approaches it, is intentionally a little fantastic. Remember his emotional tension. Once within, however, he is received with perfect courtesy according to the customs of the times. I doubt whether one can get anywhere a better notion than is given here of life in a medieval castle.

Pp. 162-185. The reader should not fail to notice, throughout this third part, the undercurrent of apprehension in Gawain's mind. Never was man more sorely tried. He was facing certain death if he kept his appointment with Green Knight; he would be recreant if he did not reach the Green Chapel on the day set, yet he was still in the dark as to how to get there; he must not fail to behave with perfect courtesy to his host's wife, yet he could not in loyalty to his host become entangled with her; he was compelled, withal, to present a gay and untroubled surface to everyone.

Pp. 187-190. Notice how the tension of the scene is increased by the fears of the guide and the roughness of weather and landscape.

P. 199. The baldric of green, as the badge of an order of knighthood, has no connection, so far as is known, with any actual group of knights. The motto at the end of the poem *Hony soyt qui mal pence* is that of the order of the Garter, but the members of it seem never to have worn a green badge.